Photographics
Photographic techniques for design

Nicholas Jenkins

Photographics

Photographic techniques for design

Nicholas Jenkins

VAN NOSTRAND REINHOLD COMPANY

NEW YORK CINCINNATI TORONTO LONDON MELBOURNE

Copyright © 1982, 1973 by Nicholas Jenkins
Library of Congress Catalog Card Number 83–12491
ISBN 0 442 24385 5

Printed in Great Britain

Van Nostrand Reinhold Company Inc.
135 West 50th Street
New York, New York 10020

15 14 13 12 11 10 9 8 7 6 5 4 3 2 1
Library of Congress Cataloging in Publication Data

Jenkins, Nicholas.
  Photographics.
  Rev. ed. of: Photo graphics. 1973.

  1. Photography, Advertising. 2. Graphic arts.
I. Title. II. Title: Photo graphics.
[TR690.4.J46 1984]   659.13′23   83–12491
ISBN 0 442 24385 (pbk.)

Contents

Author's note

This book is an introduction to some aspects of photography and phototechniques which relate to graphic design. I have made no attempt to delve into any deep cultural philosophies concerning relationships between disciplines; rather, the book is basically a description of the way in which a great deal of my own work is carried out. For this reason, I make no apologies for including so many examples of my own work.

Photo . . .

Photography in one way or another has become the everyday tool of designers; its range and potential, as a means to an image, is limitless. The continuing growth of its use to solve visual problems may be regretted by some, but it is now undeniably the designer's most valuable medium.

The camera, though not always with the benefit of film, has been in existence since the Renaissance and in the seventeenth and eighteenth centuries was often used as standard equipment by artists. Initially it was somewhat unwieldy; the camera obscura was, on occasions, as large as an entire room, with a small hole at one end through which an image of a landscape outside was projected onto the facing wall. This image could then be traced off at leisure (only interrupted, one assumes, by bad weather or nightfall). By the eighteenth century, rather more manageable 'boxes' were in use, fitted with a lens, and a ground glass viewing screen onto which the image was thrown. These later contrivances had the obvious advantage of being portable, though still not as portable as a Pentax.

A further improvement in the field of artists' aids was the camera lucida, developed by William Wollaston in 1806, which consisted of a prism, through which one could see the 'sitter', and at the same time, the paper onto which his likeness was to be drawn. Such machines were certainly useful, but obviously it was considered desirable to cut out the 'middle man' and transfer the image directly onto paper. There were many attempts to achieve this end, mostly abortive because it proved difficult to 'fix' the image. In 1717 Johann Schulze had found that a mixture of chalk, silver and nitric acid was sensitive to light and could be applied to a flat surface. Photographic images were subsequently produced by a variety of people, including Thomas

*Early sequential action pictures
taken by Eadweard Muybridge.*

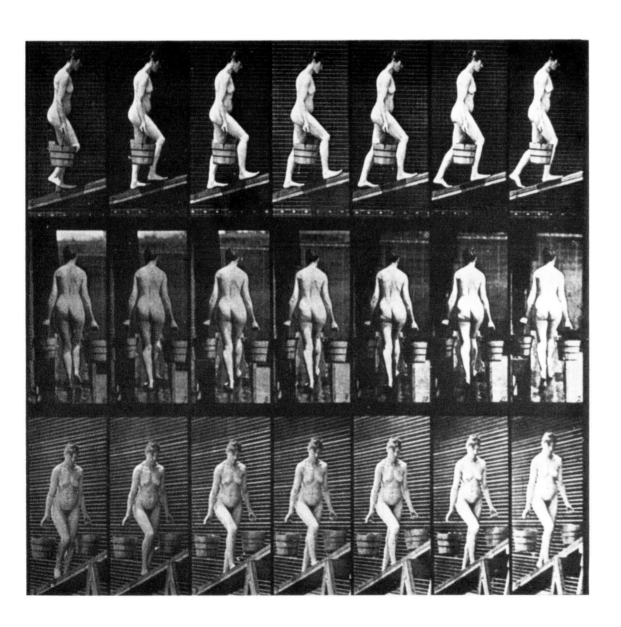

Photo . . .

Wedgwood, but the prints lasted only a few minutes. The images faded and the would-be photographers were left where they started – with a blank sheet of paper.

However, in the early 1820s, two Frenchmen, Niepce and Daguerre, working independently, managed to produce the first fixed photographic images. They worked together for a short time before Niepce's death in 1833, but it was Daguerre who finally put photography on the map. His Daguerreotypes swept the western world during the subsequent twenty years, becoming a kind of mass art-substitute.

The Daguerreotype had certain disadvantages. The image was printed on a metal plate and was therefore clumsy and difficult to carry around; the surface was very easily damaged and could not be replaced (i.e. it was a one-off process). Fox Talbot, working in England at the same time as Daguerre, managed to produce the first fixed photographs to be printed on paper. The first examples were distressingly fuzzy, due mainly to poor paper quality, but gradually the whole idea took off and all but replaced the Daguerreotype as a means of popular portraiture. By the 1860s Americans and Europeans were queuing up for their brown stereotyped portraits, printed on small bits of card.

The invention of the negative/positive process, and the fact that photographs could now be printed on paper, opened up an entirely new field of art. In addition to the mass-produced portrait, photographic 'paintings', strongly influenced by Dutch seventeenth-century painting, were turned out with speed and minimum skill with which brushes and canvas could not hope to compete. In 1853 Sir William Newton, a court painter of the time, suggested that the

*Magazine cover by Franco
Grignani.*

Photo . . .

photographic image could be manipulated by changing the negative in some way, or by using more than one negative to produce a combination print. In fact, combination printing was essential to produce a convincing exterior shot: the emulsions then in use were over-sensitive to blue and so two married negatives, taken at different exposures, had to be used to produce anything but a blank, dead white sky.

This technique soon led to complicated combination pictures, based largely on the ideas of the Pre-Raphaelite painters, sometimes using over thirty negatives for one print. For a time, until the 1880s, photography was regarded as a short cut to painting and generally speaking the results were aesthetically as bad (or as good) as the popular art form from which it drew its inspiration. However, from the 1880s onwards, a gradual awareness of the potentialities in photography as an individual art form were engendered by Peter Emerson in England and somewhat later, and perhaps more importantly, by Alfred Stieglitz in America, whose work led directly to Cartier-Bresson and Bill Brandt.

Despite advances in the technology of cameras and steady improvement of film quality, the fundamentals of photography have not changed since Fox Talbot; some kind of film or plate has always been necessary to produce an image, coupled with a chemical process for developing and printing. However, a totally new concept is now a viable proposition in the form of a video still camera. The system does not employ film, but instead translates visual images into electronic signals which are then recorded onto a small magnetic disc. Because there is no film, there is no need for the developing and printing processes which are essential to conventional photography. The

ALMEIDA THEATRE COMPANY
The left luggage room
Caledonian Hotel, Rutland Street
Edinburgh

BRITISH PREMIERE OF
TWILIGHT:ZONE
La Nuit Juste Avant les Forets by
BERNARD-MARIE KOLTES
English version by
PETER COX

TREVOR LAIRD Actor
PIERRE AUDI Director

Tickets £1.25
August 15-September 5
Incl Suns; Excl Mons Aug 24 & 31
Nightly 10 pm

Theatre poster printed in three colour line and the continuous tone photograph from which the artwork was prepared.

Photo . . .
. . . Graphics

recorded pictures can be viewed immediately on a TV set, transmitted over a telephone, dubbed onto video tape or printed onto paper.

The implications of this breakthrough are limitless, and should completely revolutionize an industry which has hitherto tended to be somewhat complacent in terms of any fundamental technological advance.

Illustration page 9   The sequential action pictures taken by Eadwaerd Muybridge in the early days of photography, though taken ostensibly to further biological research into human and animal movements (much of his work sponsored by Penn University, USA), foreshadowed not only the movies but also much graphic and photographic work done today.

. . . Graphics   The beginnings of graphic design as such are somewhat obscure; if graphic design means 'design for print', then Gutenberg and Caxton could well be regarded as among the first graphic designers, at any rate in the typographical sense. Though Henri Toulouse-Lautrec and his contemporaries in Paris were producing lithographic posters in the 1890s which were close to our concept of graphic design, it was the Beggarstaffs (James Pryde and William Nicholson) who, working in London at the same time as Lautrec in Paris, produced the first 'graphic design' posters as we now understand the term. Lautrec's posters were to some extent printed fine art, whereas the Beggarstaffs, who were both painters, established the whole concept of graphic design as a separate discipline with its own standards and aesthetics. After the initial brilliant start, graphic design tended to go downhill until the 1920s, falling prey to any kind of influence thrown up by the frenetic changes in the early twentieth century modern art scene.

In the early 1920s, as a result of constructivist and other influences,

POSTERS
BY NICHOLAS JENKINS

ROYAL COLLEGE OF ART, KENSINGTON GORE, LONDON SW7
TUES 24 JUNE – FRI 4 JULY. 10AM – 5.30 (CLOSED SAT & SUN)

Exhibition poster printed in three colour line and vignetted half tone. The stripes within the lettering and on the paint tube label are blue and green.

. . . Graphics

the Bauhaus introduced new directions into graphics, not least of which was the successful use of photography in their designs and their experiments with phototechniques. Photography had always been linked to printing in some way, if not to design; Daguerreotypes, photogravure, photolithography and photoglyphic engravings were all processes in use before 1880. The problem up until that time was that although photographs could be reproduced in quantity, they could not be printed at the same time as type, as there were no raised surfaces on the plates as in letterpress printing.

In the 1880s the Levy half-tone system and the half-tone plate were invented, revolutionizing the production of books, magazines, newspapers – in fact every printed item. As the process improved, as did photography itself, the graphic possibilities became evident. As early as 1886, a French magazine published a series of consecutive photographs of an interview, rather like an arrested movie, giving a visual immediacy to the text which would otherwise have been impossible; multiple picture essays were published; new lay-out ideas started to appear. Eventually most magazines were composed entirely of photographs, with only one- or two-line captions beneath them. Finally the whole thing started to get out of hand and an inevitable reaction set in; by the end of the First World War, magazines and newspapers were carrying feature articles and written news reports of some length, and photographs tended to give way to drawings.

In 1936 *Life* magazine first appeared. Its publisher, Henry Luce, had a new concept for the use of photography. Instead of the arbitrary and haphazard use of photographs with minimal captions as had previously been the case, the photographs would be specially commissioned to tell some specific story. In fact, a graphic essay with

Book jacket printed in three colours
with a dropped-off background.

definite direction. This is still the standard attitude in most magazines today. Photography is used to communicate and is rarely published for its own sake. In the same way, designers found that they could use photography as a compelling and immediate visual image, not only in its 'straight' form, but also by exploiting the enormous range of phototechniques, many of which were pioneered by men like Moholy-Nagy at the Bauhaus or by the 'fine art' photographers of the 1920s such as Man Ray.

Nowadays graphic design is inextricably bound up with photography. Nearly all printing depends on some photographic process which has in itself progressively influenced the conceptual thinking of graphic designers. Though it is a fear often voiced, the designer's individual stylistic possibilities have not necessarily been lost in the transition form 'hand done' to mechanical techniques. The graphic image originally conceived by the Beggarstaffs in terms of drawing might be said to have been superseded by the photodistortions of Grignani.

Illustration page 11

Basic photography

'Photo graphics', then, is not by any means a new discipline; it is simply a method, like drawing, of translating a visual concept into graphic terms. The fact that the various phototechniques exist at all is in itself a foundation for a way of thinking. Artists, from Picasso to Warhol, have been influenced by phototechniques; they, in their turn, have re-influenced graphic design. Seurat, with his pointilliste ideas on forming colour by using dots of component colours in close proximity, anticipated the four-colour printing process. That, in its turn, when 'blown-up' out of its normal scale, has often been the basis for both fine art and graphic design images. Magritte and other Surrealists have exerted enormous influence on contemporary 'ideas'

Theatre poster printed in black only. The three hands are produced from the same original by manipulating exposures.

OXFORD PLAYHOUSE
The University Theatre
Administrator & Licencee:
Barry Sheppard
Box office tel: 41733
10 am – 7.30 pm

Oxford University
Dramatic Society presents
William Shakespeare's

TIMON OF ATHENS
Tues 22 – Sat 26 November
Performances 8 pm
Matinee Saturday 2.30 pm

graphics, mostly carried out through the medium of 'trick' photography, or photocollage; the recent emergence of the 'conversation' or set piece photography in large scale poster campaigns is reminiscent of much eighteenth-century painting. In fact the whole fine art/graphic circle is linked by photography in some form or another.

Photo graphics is to the designer what the camera obscura was to Renaissance artists – a means to an end.

Some knowledge of 'pure' photography is essential to the designer. Without it, art direction of photographers would prove difficult due to lack of rapport; realization of the potential inherent in phototechniques would be severely limited; and not by any means least, it is cheaper for the designer to take simple shots as a basis for manipulation rather than to commission a professional to do the work for him.

The camera consists of three basic controllable parts. There is an aperture through which light, and therefore the image, may pass. The dimension of the aperture can be changed thereby controlling the amount of light which is exposed on to the film. Secondly, there is a shutter, which covers the aperture, the speed of which can also be controlled; and thirdly, there is a system whereby the lens can be moved nearer or further from the film surface, enabling he photographer to focus the image. These three parts can be set in relation to each other, providing a wide range of possibilities to the photographer for any given subject.

The basic function of a lens is to converge the light rays which pass through it, throwing a sharp image on to the film. (If there were no lens in the camera, but simply a small hole, an image could be produced on to film, but it would not be sharp; the light rays would

Lecture poster in two colours. The multiple image is produced from a single original.

THE NO WORD IMAGE

**TALK / FILM / SLIDES / DISCUSSION
BY JEREMY MADDEN-SIMPSON
WITH KEATON, MEYERHOLD, MARX BROS,
LITTLE TICH, TATI, SCHLEMMER, FRED ASTAIRE,
EISENSTEIN, HAIR AND MUSIC HALL.**

**RCA LECTURE THEATRE
2.15 JUNE 4**

diverge and a blurred image would result.) The focal lengths of lenses vary, and it is generally necessary to have several interchangeable lenses to cope with different situations. A long focus lens brings a distant object nearer (though the more powerful it is, the more the feeling of perspective will be reduced). A wide angle lens will include more of the image surroundings than a normal lens, but will tend to produce distortions at the edge of the picture and will exaggerate perspective. A close-up or macro lens will enable pictures to be taken of small objects when the lens is only a short distance away. A standard lens will cope with most general photography, but as far as the designer is concerned, it will be necessary to take photographs of, say, a product of some kind, and a close-up lens will probably be essential; wide angle or long focus lenses can be useful accessories.

The size of the aperture behind the lens is calibrated in 'f' numbers; the higher the number, the smaller the aperture. By manipulating the aperture size, the depth of field can be controlled. Maximum depth can be achieved by setting the aperture at its smallest (i.e. numerically largest) 'f' stop. Conversely, subjects can be isolated by being sharper than their surroundings by having the aperture fully open (and the lens accurately focused on the subject). As the amount of light which passes through the lens is altered by changing the aperture size, the shutter speed must be adjusted to compensate, otherwise the result may be a marvellous depth of field, but no light, or a sharp isolated object which is over-exposed. A light meter is essential to calculate the ideal combination of aperture size/shutter speed for any particular light condition or image requirement. Basically the meter gives a light value which, when set for the speed of the particular film to be used (marked in ASA or DIN numbers), is

Theatre poster printed in two colours, produced from a negatived photo print and torn paper.

THE OVERGROUND THEATRE PRESENTS

THE CAPTAIN

THE STORY OF SCOTT OF THE ANTARCTIC
WRITTEN AND DEVISED BY JOHN CARROLL AND ROYCE RYTON
DIRECTED BY BERNARD GOSS
WITH NICHOLAS AMER/JANE CASSON/TONY HIGGINSON/ALAN BRYCE

JUNE 26 – 29 THURSDAY TO SUNDAY 8 PM
JULY 2 – 6 WEDNESDAY TO SUNDAY 8 PM (FRIDAY 3.15 & 8 PM)
OVERGROUND THEATRE, CLARENCE ST, KINGSTON
OPPOSITE KINGSTON STATION

TICKETS 75P/TEL 549 5893

translated into a series of combinations from which to choose. For example, if the meter reads f2 aperture, to be taken at 1/125th second shutter speed (thereby giving a small focal depth), it will also show that the same conditions will allow the photograph to be taken with an f22 aperture at 1 second exposure time, which will give a large depth of field. (In this instance, a tripod would be necessary on which to mount the camera if the f22/1 sec. combination were chosen. It is not advisable to 'hand-hold' the camera at shutter speeds of longer than 1/30th sec.).

There are two basic types of camera which incorporate the minimum requirements from a designer's point of view. 35 mm cameras, so long as they have a reasonable range of aperture sizes and shutter speeds, and have the possibility of interchangeable lenses, are probably the cheapest. Otherwise, the type of camera which takes 2¼ inch square negative (120) is probably more useful, especially when close focus studio shots of objects or products are required. One factor common to both types, however, which is more or less essential to the designer in the interest of accuracy, is a reflex lens (or at least a twin lens reflex). The reflex lens camera incorporates a mirror behind the lens which reflects the image up on to the viewfinder, enabling the image to be seen exactly as it will be exposed on to the film. When the shutter is released to take the photograph, the mirror hinges up out of the way, so that it does not block the light from reaching the film, and then returns to 'viewing' position when the shutter closes. This system is normally incorporated on the better 35 mm cameras.

The single lens reflex system is used for most 2¼ in. square (120) negative cameras, though the twin lens reflex, incorporating an extra

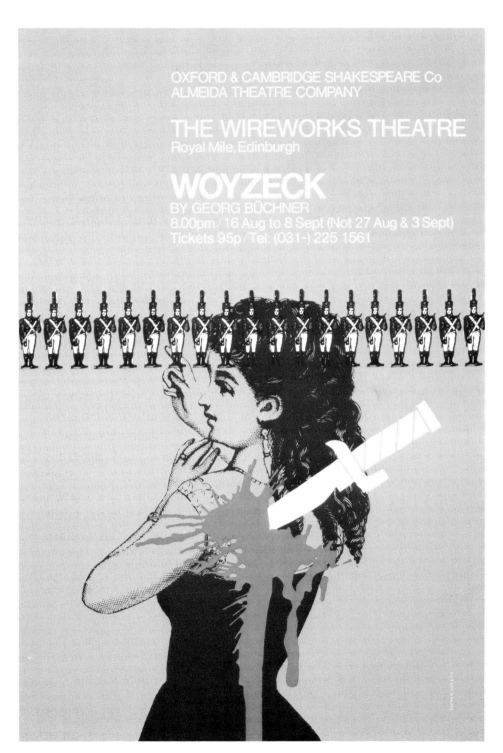

Theatre posters printed in three colours, produced from photo prints of engravings and cut paper.

lens exclusively for viewing which focuses at the same time as the main lens, is still in use. The slight disadvantage of this system is that the image seen in the viewfinder does not exactly correspond with that which is projected onto the film.

If neither of these viewing systems is used, the viewfinder will not be directly linked to the lens, and the photograph will be unreliably framed.

The type of film used in the camera can have considerable effect on the final result. As mentioned earlier, films have an ASA or DIN speed (i.e. degree of sensitivity) and it is necessary to compensate for this on a light meter before taking a reading. A fast film, say 1000 ASA, is suitable for bad light conditions or when a fast moving image needs to be 'frozen'; a relatively slow film, say 100 ASA, could be used when a subject needs isolating by limited depth of field in bright conditions or a blurred effect is desirable. Fast film has a 'grainier' quality than slow film, which can be turned to advantage as a particular effect, but if very fine definition is needed, slow film should be used. Also, more contrast can be obtained from slow film. Worth mentioning here is the polaroid land film, which is normally used in a special camera (not expensive) or can be used in interchangeable back attachments on some more sophisticated cameras. This type of film is self-developing and prints can be produced a few seconds after the photograph is taken, without going near a dark room. For the designer, this can be especially useful when art-directing a photographer, as one can have more or less instant 'proof' pictures before being committed to the final shot. For the photographer, it is especially useful for assessing quality and intensity of studio flash. It is now possible to obtain polaroid cine film, 10×8 in. colour print film

*Enlarged area of a conventional
half-tone screen and a distorted dot
screen pattern.*

and film that produces a negative.

Studio still life work is the most likely area of photography to be used to any great extent by the designer. The art director of a magazine would normally commission professional photographers to take editorial photographs such as fashion or interior shots, but a photograph of an object such as a gun or a musical instrument, eventually to be used in a more graphic form on a book jacket or record sleeve, would normally be taken by the designer himself. (The cost of commissioning a photographer to take such pictures is usually out of proportion to the designer's fee for the finished work.)

Ideally, the studio should be light proof, so that the artificial light can be exactly controlled. Also, there should be some provision for hanging large rolls of 'Colorama' paper, so that a totally flat background can be set up by dropping the paper down in a gradual curve from the vertical to the horizontal. If lit correctly, the subject can thus be isolated from its background, avoiding 'painting out' problems on the final print. In order to achieve soft, overall lighting, the walls should be painted matt white, as this enables light from floods to be 'bounced' from the walls themselves, rather than having to set up special screens for the purpose. When lighting the subject, spots, floods, etc. should be positioned first of all without the camera. (It can be extremely inhibiting and laborious to work through the viewfinder from the outset.) It is often useful to have a stock of large sheets of white card available, as these can be used to reflect light locally on to the subject to achieve the desired effects. Once the contrasts, shadow elimination or whatever, have been achieved by 'eye', the camera viewfinder should be used to make fine adjustments of both lighting and subject position relative to the camera. A light

Series of screens which can be used
as an alternative to the
conventional dot system.

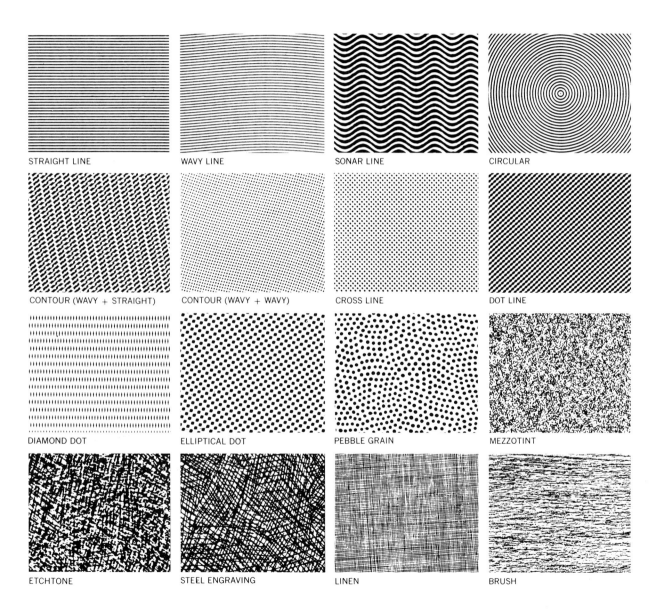

STRAIGHT LINE   WAVY LINE   SONAR LINE   CIRCULAR

CONTOUR (WAVY + STRAIGHT)   CONTOUR (WAVY + WAVY)   CROSS LINE   DOT LINE

DIAMOND DOT   ELLIPTICAL DOT   PEBBLE GRAIN   MEZZOTINT

ETCHTONE   STEEL ENGRAVING   LINEN   BRUSH

meter *must* be used to calculate the correct aperture/shutter speed. If, as is probable in a studio, a tripod is being used, then a far wider choice of combinations is available than if shooting in normal light with a hand-held camera. Being able to expose for, say, one second, even the smallest aperture can be used, thereby giving a greater depth of field. If, however, flash lighting is used, then a special flash meter will be necessary.

Some form of artificial lighting is always necessary when taking studio shots, and some systems can be very expensive. Most cameras are equipped with fixtures for flash attachments, and a flash gun can be bought fairly cheaply. Flash guns tend to produce an extremely hard light unless the gun is pointed away from the subject and on to a white surface which will reflect and diffuse the light. A far better system for studio use is an electronic flash attached to a power pack which pushes out a powerful flash for the duration of the exposure (perhaps only 1/1000th sec.). The light can be diffused by being bounced off the inside of a white umbrella, which is attached to the light source mounting. Also in the flash mounting, it is usual to have a comparatively low-powered tungsten lamp, which is lit during the setting up of the photograph, enabling the subject to be seen with the same shadows and light distribution as will occur when the flash is fired. The whole electronic flash unit can be expensive, but the tubes need replacing infrequently.

Satisfactory constant light sources can be achieved from tungsten flood or spotlights. Photoflood lamps with a bowl reflector give out a soft even light; spotlights give much more intense light, and some can be focused with a lens, giving a range of light varying from a broad hard beam to a smaller intense beam. Floods and spots can be used in

Speedwriting Shorthand

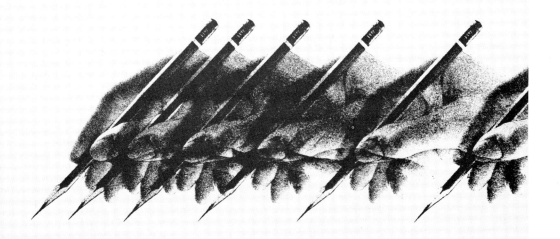

Speed Dictation 50-120wpm

conjunction: a spot to bring out detail and a flood to reduce the hard shadows produced by an intensive beam.

A tripod must be used to support the camera when copying flat artwork, as the camera lens must be positioned exactly in the centre of the subject to avoid distortions; also, care should be taken to place the artwork on an exactly vertical plane. Flat diffuse lighting should be used, the sources positioned at an angle of 45 degrees pointing towards the centre; a matt black background will avoid any glare or uneven reflections. The exposure should be calculated by taking an *average* reading across dark and light areas.

If polaroid land film equipment is available, it is advisable to take test shots to check the exposure. Several shots should be taken at speeds immediately less and more than the average meter reading. Normal panchromatic film, i.e. HP5, is suitable for recording a wide range of tones, such as would occur in multi-coloured originals; line film should be used if the subject is typography or a line drawing.

A light-proof room with ventilation, hot and cold running water with a mixer tap, a large sink, ceiling lights, two benches, cupboards, an electric clock calibrated in seconds, and power points will be necessary for film processing (though it is possible to develop film in a light-proof processing tank, in which case only a dark cupboard in which to load the film will be necessary).

The dark room should be divided into wet and dry areas. In the wet area the correct temperature of the various solutions necessary for processing can be maintained by standing the developing tanks in a shallow sink partially filled with warm water (about 20°C; 68°F). The tanks contain one or more stainless steel spirals onto which the film is rolled, and can have a light-proof funnel through which the solutions

Magazine cover printed in two colour line, the hand image being a mezzotint.

may be poured while in normal light (though the film must be wound onto the spirals in complete darkness).

The solutions for developing black and white film consist of developer and acid fixers. Once the film has been transferred from either a cassette (in the case of 35 mm) or a roll (2¼ inch or 120 film) onto a developing-spiral, the spiral is then inserted into the developing-tank and warm water poured into it. This should be gently agitated for about 30 seconds and then emptied. The developer, which should have been warmed, is then poured into the tank and agitated according to the manufacturer's instructions. (The time during which the film should be in contact with the developer will vary according to conditions such as solution temperature and type of film.) The developer can then be returned to its container for re-use and the film thoroughly rinsed in water before the fixer is used.

Fixer should be at about the same temperature as the developer and should remain in contact with the film for at least ten minutes. The film should then be washed under running water for thirty minutes, after which it can be hung up to dry (either in a special drying cabinet or, for a longer period, in a dust-free room). In the case of pure black and white subject matter, such as typography artwork, a special 'line' or high-contrast developer can be used, which eliminates all mid-tones from the negative. Some degree of correction can be achieved after the film is developed by immersing it in a 'reducer' solution if the negative is too dense (which will tend to increase contrast). The action of the reducer can be controlled by immersing the film in water, which will arrest its action. If the negative is too 'thin' or more graininess is required, an 'intensifier' solution can be used. This initially bleaches the negative, after which it will need re-developing,

Theatre poster; both figures produced from the same original.

causing the blacks to become more dense.

If the whole procedure of film developing seems laborious, there are plenty of local stores who will oblige; however, in the end, it will prove more expensive, in addition to which no control can be exercised over the final negative.

The same darkroom as described above can be used for printing, with the addition of an enlarger (to be placed on a dry area bench), some dishes to contain various print sizes, orange safelights under which most work is carried out, and the appropriate chemicals and containers. An enlarger consists basically of a light source, a holder for the negative and a lens with variable size aperture for focusing the negative image to the desired size on to the base board.

The simplest function this apparatus can perform is to make contact prints by directing an even beam of light (with the aperture wide open) on to a negative sandwiched between sensitized paper and a sheet of glass on the base board.

To make an enlargement, the negative is placed in the negative carrier and light directed through it on to a white card on the base board in order that the projected image can be exactly focused. The aperture should be fully open while focusing to allow for maximum light and therefore clarity. The size of the image can be altered by moving the whole enlarger up or down on its mounting. When the projected image is judged to be the right size and sharply focused, photographic paper is placed on the base board, emulsion side up, and the enlarger stopped down to allow an exposure of about ten seconds. The amount of 'stopping down' required will depend on the density or otherwise of the negative and is best determined by trial exposures on small test strips of photographic paper before the final exposure.

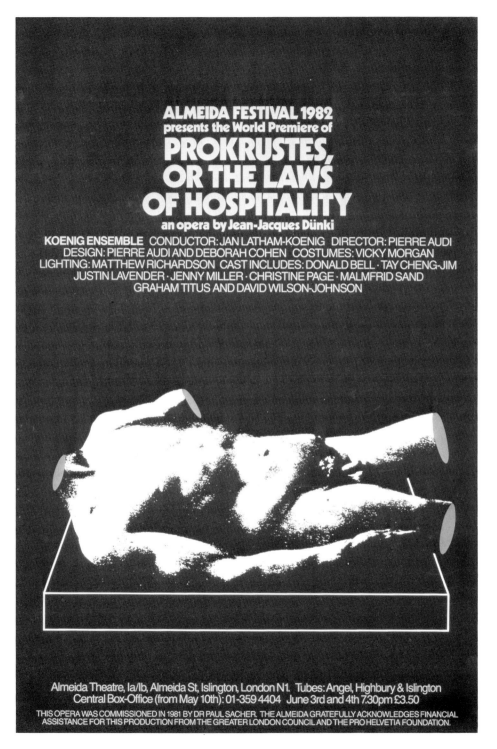

ALMEIDA FESTIVAL 1982
presents the World Premiere of

PROKRUSTES, OR THE LAWS OF HOSPITALITY

an opera by Jean-Jacques Dünki

KOENIG ENSEMBLE CONDUCTOR: JAN LATHAM-KOENIG DIRECTOR: PIERRE AUDI
DESIGN: PIERRE AUDI AND DEBORAH COHEN COSTUMES: VICKY MORGAN
LIGHTING: MATTHEW RICHARDSON CAST INCLUDES: DONALD BELL · TAY CHENG-JIM
JUSTIN LAVENDER · JENNY MILLER · CHRISTINE PAGE · MALMFRID SAND
GRAHAM TITUS AND DAVID WILSON-JOHNSON

Almeida Theatre, Ia/Ib, Almeida St, Islington, London N1. Tubes: Angel, Highbury & Islington
Central Box-Office (from May 10th): 01-359 4404 June 3rd and 4th 7.30pm £3.50

THIS OPERA WAS COMMISSIONED IN 1981 BY DR PAUL SACHER. THE ALMEIDA GRATEFULLY ACKNOWLEDGES FINANCIAL
ASSISTANCE FOR THIS PRODUCTION FROM THE GREATER LONDON COUNCIL AND THE PRO HELVETIA FOUNDATION.

Two companion posters employing manipulated classical images. The Prokrustes figure is Michaelangelo's David, the truncated limb ends being bright red.

Basic Photography

The procedure for print developing is similar to that used for developing negatives, but the solutions used are somewhat more active. Normally, developer should be warm (about 20°C; 68°F). Again, this temperature can be maintained by standing the containing dish in running water from the mixer tap. Developing time is normally about two minutes, after which the print should be rinsed under running water (for about the same amount of time), then placed in a fixer dish, face down, for ten minutes. A final water rinse should last for thirty minutes before hanging up to dry.

The basic procedure for printing from negatives can be extensively varied to produce an almost endless variety of results. The type of paper on which the print is made is a crucial factor. The papers most commonly used are bromide and resin coated, both available in a wide range of textures and grades. (Bromide papers, for example, are graded from 0 to 5, denoting the amount of contrast that will occur on the print). Resin coated paper has the advantage that it can be processed up to dry print stage in only four minutes, using rapid fixers, and is more widely available than bromide papers. The choice of paper for any given print might depend on compensating for an over-hard contrast, or soft negative, or to exaggerate contrast or softness. If an extremely high contrast is required (i.e. hard black or white with no intermediate tones), lith paper should be used, but it must be processed in developer used for negatives and handled under red (not orange) safelights. By using multigrade papers, prints can be produced with high contrast in one area and a soft effect in another.

Illustration page 13   The difference between using ordinary continuous tone paper and lith paper can be seen by comparing the 'straight' print of an actor's portrait and its eventual use on a poster for a play.

OVERGROUND THEATRE

Ashdown Road, Kingston
One minute from
Eden St post office

WINTER SEASON

Performances 8pm
Tickets £1
Box office 549 5893

Jan 25-Feb 5/Tuesday to Saturday
THE HAPPIEST OF THE THREE
by Eugene Labiche
The classic French farce

Feb 8-19/Tuesday to Saturday
TWO FOR THE SEESAW
by William Gibson
A bittersweet love affair

Feb 22-Mar 5/Tuesday to Saturday
ALPHA BETA
by E A Whitehead
Whitehead's masterpiece

Part of a series of posters employing single colour printing on coloured paper.

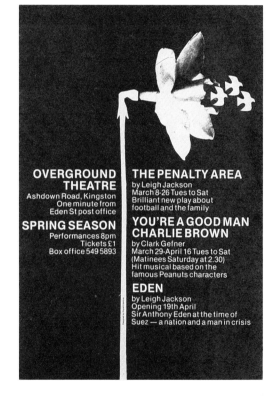

OVERGROUND THEATRE
Ashdown Road, Kingston
One minute from
Eden St post office

SPRING SEASON
Performances 8pm
Tickets £1
Box office 549 5893

THE PENALTY AREA
by Leigh Jackson
March 8-26 Tues to Sat
Brilliant new play about
football and the family

YOU'RE A GOOD MAN CHARLIE BROWN
by Clark Gefner
March 29-April 16 Tues to Sat
(Matinees Saturday at 2.30)
Hit musical based on the
famous Peanuts characters

EDEN
by Leigh Jackson
Opening 19th April
Sir Anthony Eden at the time of
Suez — a nation and a man in crisis

Basic Photography

Artwork was prepared by painting out all unwanted details on the lith paper print and, in order to introduce some degree of grain, making a straight photocopy on roughish paper. The 'rain' was produced by pasting up a number of photocopies of a small section of the overall pattern – thus saving hours of laborious artwork time.

Faces are always compelling images, having an obvious human rapport with the viewer. In this case, the play was a single-hander concerning the disillusionment of a coloured man involved in Western society. Using a portrait of the actor as the central image, his blackness emphasized by the phototechnique used, makes an immediate statement, at least on one level, about the play's subject.

Lith paper is also available with a translucent base; this can be used as a film positive for exposure direct onto silk screens. Totally transparent film bases are also available for printing, which can be useful for making artwork separation overlays, black and white slides for projection or as a step in producing a solarized print. (If the print is briefly exposed to white light during its development, the tones tend partially to reverse and a strange outline effect occurs. The result, if on a transparent base, can then be contact-printed on to film, thus producing a negative from which paper prints can be taken. The process can be performed with ordinary bromide paper but with rather less control.)

In addition to paper and film, it is possible to produce a photographic image on almost any material by spraying the surface with sensitized emulsion. Timber or brick prints, though somewhat unwieldy, are at least practical possibilities.

At the developing end of the process, prints can be intensified or bleached by application of chemicals (i.e. Farmers reducer or iodine

Part of a series of posters employing full colour cut out images.

Furniture catalogue cover employing minimal use of full colour.

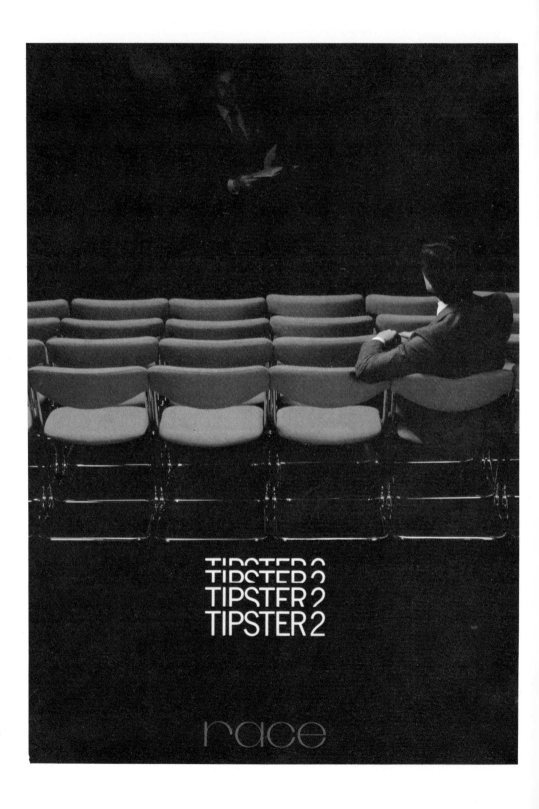

Johnsen & Jorgensen Ltd
Service and development
in glass and plastic containers

Brochure cover exploiting the colour subtleties in glass.

Photographic poster using exaggerated perspective.

Spectator's Choice

KINGSLEY AMIS / ALAN BRIEN / D.W. BROGAN / ANTHONY BURGESS
ELIZABETH DAVID / PETER FLEMING / ROBERT RHODES JAMES
GRAHAM GREENE / COLIN MACINNES / IAIN MACLEOD / NANCY MITFORD
SIMON RAVEN / ANDREW SINCLAIR / EVELYN WAUGH

Edited by George Hutchinson

Book jacket using a combination of a line derivative photoprint, a dot screen overlay and separated drawing.

bleacher) or the blacks on a print can be coloured by bleaching a fully developed print and redeveloping it in a colour toner. This can be done overall, or only on specific areas of the print. Partially fogging prints (briefly exposing to white light) during development can produce weird effects (but startling quantities of paper may be used up during this rather uncontrollable hit-or-miss process).

Image Isolation   The designer will often require a photographic image to be isolated from its background or to have a 'non-background'. This can be done by masking areas of the negative on the enlarger or by interfering with the projected beam between the enlarger lens and the print. There are other methods, however, performed after the print is made, which in certain circumstances can be more precise. When a continuous tone photographic image is transferred to a printing block or plate for reproduction, a half-tone process is employed whereby the image is 'screened' (i.e. broken up into a dot system or varying intensity which tonally corresponds to the original).

Illustration page 15   The poster for an exhibition (showing a tube of poster colour) is from a continuous tone photograph printed half-tone, with most of the background painted out on the film positive from which the printing plate was made. (Even if the original photograph had a dead white background, some dot tone would inevitably be picked up during the screening process). In this case, the image would have stood out less if all the background tone had been left on, producing a grey, and probably uneven, overall texture.

In order to avoid a possibly clumsy and contrived image which might have resulted if all the background tone had been removed, some shadow has been retained, lending presence and a sense of place to the image. Very careful lighting was necessary when taking the

Fire

Flaming, flickering,
brilliant diamonds
restlessly dancing to the
music of time

'Vendôme'–a white gold and diamond
watch from the Les Must de Cartier range.
£2,000 to £4,500.

*Full page advertisement
marrying two photographs
together.*

47

Image Isolation

original photograph in order to achieve the right degree of tone and shape to the shadow. Clear specifications should always be given to the printer if the background tone is to be left off. In the case of a cut-out image, the exact area to be isolated should be marked on an overlay. If there are areas which need to be graded from tone to dead white (vignette), the exact area across which this tonal reduction is to take place should be clearly defined. Vignetting can be a somewhat hazardous procedure, and can go badly wrong; when printed, ink coagulation can occur at the dot-tone area extremities, forming an ugly outline around what is meant to be a delicate tone grade. Generally vignettes should be avoided unless great confidence can be placed in the printer.

The 'poster' poster was printed in three colour line and tone, the alternate blue and green stripes in the typography being echoed on the paint tube label.

Illustration page 17   The wrap-around jacket for a book on Eadweard Muybridge has a 'cut-out' image which was achieved by a combination of artwork and line re-photography. The original photograph, taken in the latter part of the last century, was in poor condition. Spots, blodges and marks of all kinds covered not only the background (which was originally white) but the figures themselves. To prepare artwork for the jacket, the background was painted out on the print to flat white, maintaining the soft edge of the figures caused by the grain in the original, by simulating a grain edge with a fine brush. The blemishes on the figures themselves had to be blocked out in white and a grain texture as similar as possible to the surrounding areas applied to the figures. Because the grain was exceedingly coarse on the original (thereby breaking up the image in a similar way to a half-tone screen)

GEOFIT TABLES

A single line photoprint overprinted twice in two colours.

Image Isolation
Colour

it was possible to specify a line treatment for the printing (i.e. no screening); this eliminated the problem of painting out any background tone that would have picked up on the film positive if shot half-tone, at the same time maintaining a continuous tone appearance to the printed image.

Colour   All the procedures mentioned so far have largely been concerned with black and white photography. Although colour photographs are basically no more difficult to take providing light sources are not mixed (i.e.: natural/artificial), the processing and manipulation of colour is far more complex and, so far as the designer is concerned, it is more convenient to specify requirements to a laboratory. However, the choice of film is an important factor and depends on the subject (daylight or artificial lighting) and the form in which the final result will appear (print or transparency).

In terms of original artwork, colour transparencies should be used in preference to colour prints on paper if the image is to be produced in four colour half-tone printing. (Colour and tonal values are truer and the image is usually sharper. However, as there is no negative involved (transparencies are produced from colour reversal film), the artwork cannot normally be duplicated by the traditional photographic printing process without an extra negative (inter-negative) being made from the transparency itself. For example, if a colour paper print is required from a colour transparency (this might arise when presenting a colour rough to a client and the transparency is intended for final block- or plate-making after approval), the transparency will have to be rephotographed on to colour negative film and then printed on paper. There will be some loss of quality, due to the number of stages through which the original must pass before

Photographs for a furniture brochure implying 'presence' without the use of elaborate sets or models.

Colour

the print is produced.

There is however a process which can obviate this problem, whereby colour prints can be made directly through an enlarger from transparencies. This involves special paper and chemicals (Cibachrome), but on the whole the results are somewhat short on tonal range. However, it is a useful short cut method and can prove extremely useful for the designer.

Paper prints will obviously be of a higher quality if produced directly from colour negative film. They should be used for presentation layouts if a final artwork photograph can be taken at a later stage on reversal film, or if artwork needs to be worked directly on to the photograph by hand.

A further consideration when choosing the type of colour film to be used is whether the colour balance is to be for daylight or artificial light. (Colour reversal and colour negative film are available in both categories.) Daylight film can be used with electronic flash, as well as for normal outdoor use. If used with ordinary studio lighting or domestic light, a strong orange cast will occur; conversely a strong blue cast will appear on shots taken in daylight with an artificial light film. It is possible, however, to fit an orange filter to the camera to compensate for colour bias when using an artificial light film in daylight, but the results are never as good as when using the correct film. Mixed light sources (i.e. a studio-lit subject with some daylight) should always be avoided.

As with black and white film, colour film is available in various speeds (ASA rating), but the general range is lower. The best results, in terms of definition and sharpness, will be obtained from very low-speed films (ASA 25); the higher speeds (ASA 1000) produce low

Brochure cover; full cover photograph taken with a smeared lens.

Colour

contrasts, high grain and some loss of colour quality.

There are several types of colour film available, other than those described above, which produce special or unusual effects: infra-red film will produce strange colour reversals, red will show yellow, most greens will come out red, but blue remains blue; very high contrast colour film, normally used for copying line artwork, can produce 'block tone' colour effects when used for multi-tone subjects; as with black and white film, colour film is obtainable for use with a polaroid camera (instant prints).

It remains to be noted that colour photography is expensive; a really first class colour print on paper can cost as much as five times the price of a black and white print; on the other hand, it is difficult for the designer to present his exact intention to the client if colour photography is involved without going to this expense. It is usually unwise to sell an idea by saying 'it may look dull on my rough, but just wait till you see it in colour'. The designer should be the visualizer, not the client.

The use of full colour photography on posters is a normal and accepted procedure adopted by advertising agencies. Highly imaginative and effective campaigns have been produced in this way for many years – the photographs usually serving the concept rather than being used for their own sake; for this reason, tight art direction is essential not only to ensure accurate visual translation of the idea, but also because the end product must be a compelling overall concept, successfully marrying typography to image.

Conversely, the designer faced with the problem of creating posters from ready-made images, (as in the case of an exhibition, where the exhibits, if to be illustrated, are what they are and should not be

A series of symbols, produced by simple distortions under a process camera.

Colour

tampered with) needs to find a way to balance the visual dynamic required of a poster with reverence for the object to be used.

Illustration page 41 The posters for 'The Great Japan Exhibition' employ the use of full colour cut-out photographs of various objects and details from a large selection of exhibits ranging from screen paintings to swords, kimonos, masks and objects of all kinds. The problem was fourfold. Firstly, to depict the range of objects on show; secondly, as the exhibition was in two parts, to ring the changes halfway through the exhibition; thirdly, there were two sizes of poster sites available (30×20in and 60×40in) with insufficient funds available for two sets of origination and printing; fourthly, revenue from the sale of posters at the exhibition was needed to cover the production costs.

The solution was to design two 60×40in composite posters, one for each part of the exhibition, in such a way that they could be guillotined into four single 30×20in posters. This produced a range of eight for sale, while obviating the necessity for separate originations for the smaller size.

In order that the visual structure worked for each poster in relation to the others, images had to be selected which had a similar weight and mass, but nevertheless represented the broad scope of the exhibition.

A large painting will not easily relate to, say, a mask or a fan. For this reason, details were selected from the more complex works which related spatially to the more useable objects.

At the stage at which the posters were designed, only 5×4 in transparencies were available, the objects themselves being at that time in various collections throughout the world. Any considerations of scale were therefore abandoned (as actual sizes were unknown) in

Process camera distortions and manipulation of focus and depth of field.

TYPOGRAPHY

TYPOGRAPHY

TYPOGRAPHY

TYPOGRAPHY

TYPOGRAPHY   *TYPOGRA*

TYPOGRAPHY

TYPOGRAPHY

TYPOGRAPHY

Colour
Presentations

favour of graphic balance.

Colour is a highly complex subject, both from the technical and psychological viewpoints. It can be emotive, symbolic, decorative, compelling or, if handled insensitively, just gaudy. Leonardo Da Vinci related colours to the elements: yellow for earth, green for water, blue for air, red for fire. Others have put forward different associations. Transport authorities, for example, have decided that red means stop and green means go. 'Purple with rage', 'green with envy', 'blue with cold' are all emotive linguistic expressions which have a bearing on our perception of colour. Colour photography and the use of colour in graphics should not be arbitrary – colours have their own symbolism which can be exploited in any communications medium.

Illustration page 42

If full-colour printing is available it can, paradoxically, work to advantage by being used only minimally. The cover for a furniture brochure employs the simple technique of photographing a brightly coloured product in a monochromatic environment – even the models have black suits and white shirts. If other colours had been introduced, the impact of the total image would have been

Illustration page 43

proportionally reduced. Likewise, the brochure cover for a glass and plastics manufacturer uses full colour sparingly, the dominant theme being white. Glass has its own subtle colours and, if lit correctly, needs no enhancement.

Presentations Perhaps the easiest way for a designer to present both his own work and a specific project to a client, is by projecting everything on 35 mm colour slides. A camera with a close-up lens and the use of a well-equipped photographic studio with good lighting facilities is necessary for such photography, as uneven lighting or unsharp pictures can easily negate the value of the exercise. The main advantage of this

Magazine spread employing
overlaid full colour photographs.

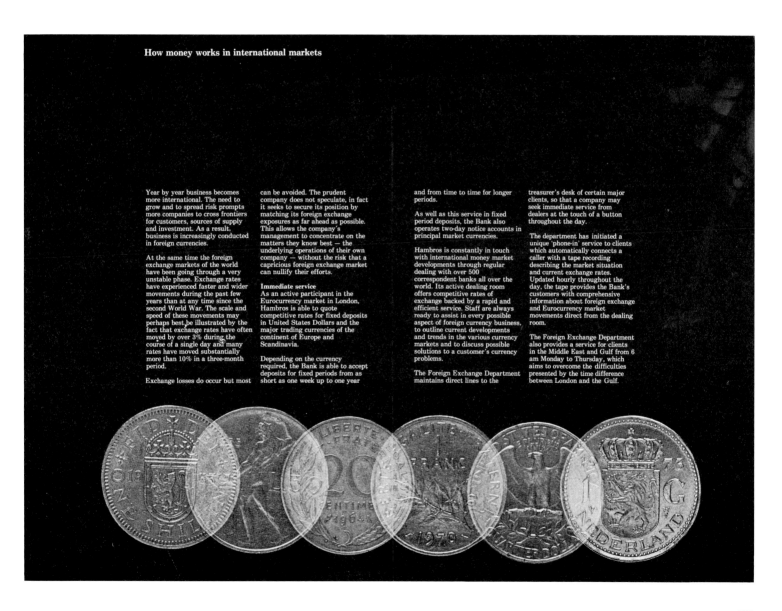

How money works in international markets

Year by year business becomes more international. The need to grow and to spread risk prompts more companies to cross frontiers for customers, sources of supply and investment. As a result, business is increasingly conducted in foreign currencies.

At the same time the foreign exchange markets of the world have been going through a very unstable phase. Exchange rates have experienced faster and wider movements during the past few years than at any time since the second World War. The scale and speed of these movements may perhaps best be illustrated by the fact that exchange rates have often moved by over 3% during the course of a single day and many rates have moved substantially more than 10% in a three-month period.

Exchange losses do occur but most can be avoided. The prudent company does not speculate, in fact it seeks to secure its position by matching its foreign exchange exposures as far ahead as possible. This allows the company's management to concentrate on the matters they know best — the underlying operations of their own company — without the risk that a capricious foreign exchange market can nullify their efforts.

Immediate service
As an active participant in the Eurocurrency market in London, Hambros is able to quote competitive rates for fixed deposits in United States Dollars and the major trading currencies of the continent of Europe and Scandinavia.

Depending on the currency required, the Bank is able to accept deposits for fixed periods from as short as one week up to one year

and from time to time for longer periods.

As well as this service in fixed period deposits, the Bank also operates two-day notice accounts in principal market currencies.

Hambros is constantly in touch with international money market developments through regular dealing with over 500 correspondent banks all over the world. Its active dealing room offers competitive rates of exchange backed by a rapid and efficient service. Staff are always ready to assist in every possible aspect of foreign currency business, to outline current developments and trends in the various currency markets and to discuss possible solutions to a customer's currency problems.

The Foreign Exchange Department maintains direct lines to the

treasurer's desk of certain major clients, so that a company may seek immediate service from dealers at the touch of a button throughout the day.

The department has initiated a unique 'phone-in' service to clients which automatically connects a caller with a tape recording describing the market situation and current exchange rates. Updated hourly throughout the day, the tape provides the Bank's customers with comprehensive information about foreign exchange and Eurocurrency market movements direct from the dealing room.

The Foreign Exchange Department also provides a service for clients in the Middle East and Gulf from 6 am Monday to Thursday, which aims to overcome the difficulties presented by the time difference between London and the Gulf.

method of presentation is that the viewer is held captive at the discretion of the presenter by whatever image appears on the screen. This is especially useful when presenting a large range of related objects, for example a corporate identity programme, as the client will not be diverted by aspects of the job which are not relevant to the particular point being made at the time. In a case such as this, when it is likely that many of the items for presentation will vary considerably in size, a sense of scale needs to be preserved. For example, if the largest item to be shown is a poster, then a letter heading must not appear the same size on the screen.

Audio-visual presentations are now being increasingly used for communicating concepts or presenting complex design proposals to clients. Computer-controlled multiple projection and stereo sound can result in an impressive show, using straightforward 35 mm slides.

Another more obvious advantage of a portfolio of transparencies is that it can be transported. If the designer is lucky enough to have clients in Los Angeles and Tokyo, or Paris and Milan, his entire work can be sent in an envelope, rather than being trussed up in a packing case.

In some instances, it may be worth considering using movie or video in conjunction with slides, especially when showing an identity scheme applied to vans and shopfronts. A simple 8mm movie, or a held-held video camera is usually adequate for this purpose.

PMT machines   In addition to the conventional photographic equipment already mentioned, one of the most versatile alternatives as far as the designer is concerned (which does not cost a fortune) is a process camera linked to an automatic single bath processor. The camera is a kind of upside down enlarger, with a moveable lens and copy board lit

Images produced by a distorting camera

PMT machines

by halogen lamps, with a horizontal glass screen on to which the image is thrown. Its basic function is to enlarge or diminish any image placed on the copy board.

Images are produced by the photo mechanical transfer (PMT) method; negative paper is placed over the projected image on the viewing screen, exposed for the requisite time and fed through the automatic processor face to face with positive film or paper.

Exposure times depend on the degree of enlargement or reduction required, and are automatically shown on the machine itself.

Illustration page 19 However, by manipulating the exposure, certain effects can be achieved, as on the *Timon of Athens* poster. The hand image is made to progressively 'decay' by underexposing the original print in two stages.

Continuous tone, line derivative (hard prints which reduce all greys to either black or white) or negative prints are obtainable by using appropriate grades of paper. The system is simple, requiring no specialist knowledge of photography or phototechniques. The possibilities inherent in this comparatively simple set-up are endless; images can be blurred by throwing the focus out of true, or by moving the negative across the viewing screen whilst exposing. This latter technique can produce an effective impression of movement or speed. In the preparation of artwork, especially where a number of different elements have to be sized or collated into one integrated image, the system is both quick and cheap to operate.

A major problem which continually confronts the designer is how to produce presentation roughs to the client, which appear as much like a finished printed job as possible. The process camera has the advantage of being able to produce a clean print, which can be pasted

Distortions made with optical
overlay units.

Neue Möglichkeiten der Grafik
KREATIVE GESTALTUNG MIT DER KAMERA

PMT machines

on to a layout, of various elements where all edges and cut marks can be eliminated by using the correct exposure. Colour can then be overlaid with adhesive film or indian ink.

By using a slightly more complex procedure, self-coloured images can be produced on special film material from black and white artwork. There are currently six colours available: red, green, blue, yellow, magenta, cyan, and opaque white. The only essential additional piece of equipment required is a developing tray containing a special chemical into which the film is immersed after normal development in the automatic processor.

This facility opens up great scope for producing highly finished coloured visuals in the minimum amount of time. The colours are transparent, and can therefore be overlaid on each other to produce composite colours. For example, magenta + blue = purple; yellow + cyan + magenta = brown (though incidentally, a far simpler procedure for obtaining this colour is to produce a conventional black and white paper print and prematurely separate it from its negative).

Straight line prints made on the process camera can facilitate considerable image manipulation with the minimum of technical skill. The poster image – a photograph of Buster Keaton – when reduced to line, was easily 'animated'. Some of the images were produced on film and overlaid in order to achieve overprints and left to right reversals.

Black and white reversals can be achieved by using negative paper on the process camera. The poster for *The Captain*, a play about the South Pole explorer Scott, consists of a simple negative reversal of a ship's mast in conjunction with a torn paper foreground. The intended overall effect, a feeling of frozen isolation, was easily achieved by

Illustration page 21

Illustration page 23

Credit title sequence produced by distortions and collage of engravings.

spending three or four minutes on a process camera with perhaps fifteen minutes on artwork.

Illustration page 25 To some extent, the companion posters for *Far From The City* and *Woyzeck* were conceived in terms of the techniques available using the process camera system. They could have been line drawings, paintings, tone photographs or almost anything. However, the way in which they were eventually treated (collaged photo-prints taken from engravings in conjunction with cut-out shapes) depended more on the designer's individual attitude than anything else. If someone else had designed these posters, he would doubtless have come up with a totally different solution, both in conceptual and stylistic terms.

A mark made by a pencil on cartridge paper, although it may have the same form as an image exposed onto photographic paper, will nevertheless have a different character. One is not necessarily aesthetically better than the other, just more suitable for a given job, or a given designer doing that job. Design is, after all, a form of personal expression, however submerged it may sometimes appear to be. The crucial factor is how the designer uses the various means available to him and whether the final result justifies his actions.

Screens The normal method of reproducing a photograph for either letterpress or litho printing involves breaking up the original continuous tone picture into dots by means of filtering the projected image through a screen. The close-up of a section of a screened film positive shows how tonal variations are produced. The same method applies for reproducing colour photographs, except that the system is multiplied by four, one screened separation for each of the four basic colours.

By the same token, a further important facility provided by the

Opening and closing film titles employing animated photographic stills.

WOLCOTT

Director
COLIN BUCKSEY

Winston Churchill Wolcott
GEORGE WILLIAM HARRIS
Melinda Marin
CHRISTINE LAHTI

Terry Rowe
WARREN CLARKE
Reuben Warre
RAUL NEWNEY

Music
ANDY McKAY
Music copyright © MCMLXXXI
ITC Film Scores Ltd,
London, England.
All rights reserved.

Assistant Editor
DENNIS McTAGGART
Lighting by
LEE ELECTRIC
Stills
ROBERT MARSHALL
Special Effects
DAVID HARRIS
Stunt Co-ordinator
JOHN SULLIVAN
Production Accountant
JEFFREY BROOM
Titles by
GUYATT/JENKINS
Processed by
TECHNICOLOR

Associate Producer
CHRIS GRIFFIN
Art Director
MIKE PORTER

Screens

process camera system is that it is possible to tonally reduce images by means of screen filters. These are basically sheets of film placed between the negative and the viewing screen during exposure, breaking an original continuous tone image into dots, lines, or a variety of patterns. This system can also be used to reduce colour densities on film, thereby producing an infinite range of composite colours (i.e.: solid yellow + 80% magenta = orange; 60% cyan + solid yellow + 40% magenta = olive green). As this exactly reproduces normal colour printing systems, extremely accurate visuals can be produced.

The selection of any particular type of screen can be a major factor in the final appearance of an image. If too fine a screen is selected for reproduction on poor quality paper such as newsprint, the image will clog and become indistinct. If too coarse a screen is used on art paper, the dominance of the dot pattern can distract from the image. On the other hand, by deliberately using the 'wrong' screen, certain effects can be achieved which can contribute to the final image.

Illustration page 27

Illustration page 29

Conventional screens used for reproducing continuous tone images consist of a dot pattern in various densities. There are, however, numerous special effect screens available which can add graphic style to a photograph, or improve on a poor original. These range from straight or wavy lines, concentric circles or cross hatch to woodgrain, steel engraving or mezzotint.

Illustration page 31

The latter screen technique was used on the record sleeve for *Speedwriting Shorthand*. The original continuous tone photograph was converted to mezzotint onto six separate sheets of clear film. These were overlaid to produce a single image, printed in line. The

Illustration page 33

magazine cover *Adult Illiteracy* combined mezzotint (for the hand)

Film title sequence animated by a series of dissolves.

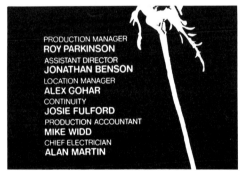

Screens
Reference
Economics

with a solid colour overlay (for the book).

Reference   It is at this point worth mentioning the importance of a comprehensive reference library. The majority of images in this book, from Captain's Scott's Ship (an engraving from a book on American nineteenth-century advertising) to the Buster Keaton image (taken from a book on movies) come from a reference collection built up over the years. The problem, if one wishes to reproduce a previously published image photographically, is that material is only free of copyright after 50 years. However, there are many commercial reference libraries which normally charge reasonable reproduction

Illustration page 35   fees, with an additional search fee. The Rosencrantz and Guildenstern figures were obtained in this way, being originally a single still from a Shakespearean production. Two simple line conversions were sized on the process camera; one on film to achieve a left to right reversal, the puppet strings being ruled up on a drawing board.

Illustration page 37   The companion posters for the Almeida Festival and a bizarre opera production of "Prokrustes" employ images from a classical art (the truncated figure is in fact Michaelangelo's David). The only practical way in which these images could have been obtained is from photographic reference; the various processes to which the original book illustrations have been subjected (PMT, photocopy, retouching) avoids the copyright problem simply by manipulating the images out of all recognition.

Economics   Production economics are a major factor in almost every job the designer is likely to handle. The designer's problem is to work within imposed economic limitations (such as only two colours) without sacrificing the quality of the job.

Illustration page 39   The limitation imposed on the series of theatre posters, for example,

Collage by John Heartfield from the 1930s.

was that they should be printed in one colour line. By using self-coloured paper and strong line derivating images, there is no feeling of cheapness in the final results.

A further possibility of squeezing more variation out of a simply printed job is to vary colour areas tonally by means of a flat dot screen. This can be easily done in the case of flat, well defined colour areas by laying down a mechanical tint (available in self-adhesive sheets) on the artwork and cutting away the unwanted areas. In the case of a line photographic image or drawing (or parts of either), they can be tonally reduced photomechanically at the printing stage. A chart showing the exact amount of tonal reduction required (i.e. 25 per cent, 50 per cent, etc.) should be used when making out the printer's specification.

Illustration page 45

The *Spectator's Choice* book jacket shows a combination of line photograph, flat dot screen and line drawing. The typewriter was photographed under a process camera to artwork size onto line paper. A self-adhesive dot screen was laid on an acetate overlay, the unwanted parts being cut away with a scalpel. The flowers were drawn on two translucent overlays (one for each colour) and the lower part of the combined flower image traced on to the typewriter line screen image to facilitate painting out a reversal into which the flowers would print. Although the printing cost was necessarily low (specified as three-colour line from same-size separated artwork), a fair degree of colour/texture variation was possible by exploiting overprinting (a fourth colour was obtained by overlapping the flowers) and the flat screen reduction of solid black (producing grey as a fifth colour).

Art direction

Straight photography is the most often-used medium for graphic

*Booklet cover combining flat cut
out and photographic detail.*

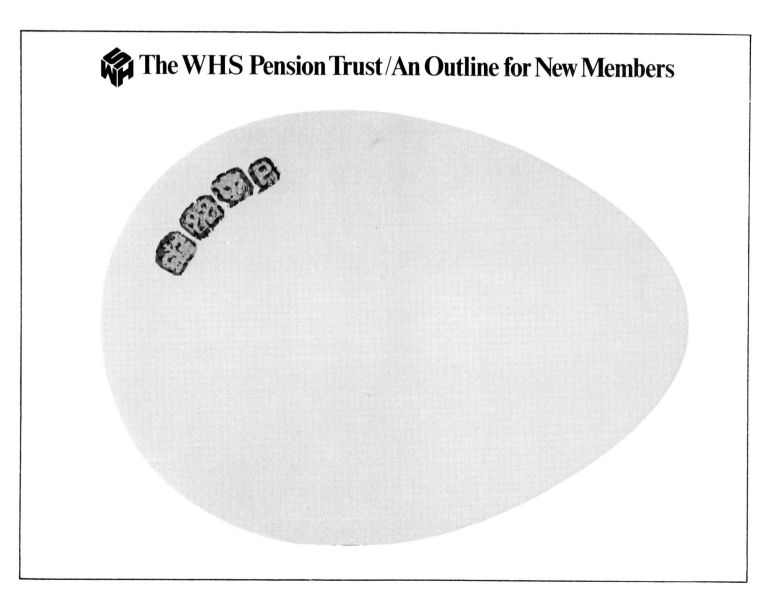

The WHS Pension Trust/An Outline for New Members

Art direction

communication in the advertising world. The designer or art director is often required to act as midwife: a kind of catalyst between the conceptual side, which includes such considerations as market research findings, group discussions etc., and the final translation of the advertising idea into visual terms by the photographer. The midwife role is a difficult one in this instance, not only from the technical point of view, where the art director needs to be fully aware of the potential (or limitations) of the available facilities (and indeed of the photographer himself), but also from a human point of view; photographers are usually creative, individualistic people and their views obviously have to be respected. Sometimes the art director can find himself uncomfortably balanced between four or five preconceptions as to how the job should look. The creative director of the agency, the client himself, and the photographer can all have differing images of the final job in mind. A further difficulty is that although one of the declared aims of the art director in advertising is originality, there are some areas of the business which work directly against this.

Due to a certain timidity or lack of confidence in the creative ability of their staff, some agencies (and for that matter some clients) tend to prefer well-tried formulae for their advertising concepts and visual solutions. For example, it is almost impossible to detect any basic difference between the approaches used to advertise one brand of lower priced cigarettes as against another. At some stage, someone came up with a formula which worked (i.e. launched a successful brand or radically increased sales) and the natural, if somewhat unadventurous assumption on the part of the rival products was that if ruched silk backgrounds work for one product, then they will work

FEBRUARY 1978
1 2 3 4 5 6 7 8 9 10 11 12 13 14 15 16 17 18 19 20 21 22 23 24 25 26 27 28

AFROTEC MOVES WITH NIGERIA   AGENTS FOR

MAY 1978
1 2 3 4 5 6 7 8 9 10 11 12 13 14 15 16 17 18 19 20 21 22 23 24 25 26 27 28 29 30 31

AFROTEC MOVES WITH NIGERIA   AGENTS FOR

*Pages from a calendar using
full colour studio shots
collaged with monochrome
catalogue photographs.*

OCTOBER 1978
1 2 3 4 5 6 7 8 9 10 11 12 13 14 15 16 17 18 19 20 21 22 23 24 25 26 27 28 29 30 31

AFROTEC MOVES WITH NIGERIA   AGENTS FOR SAMBRON

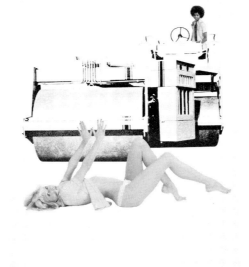

DECEMBER 1978
1 2 3 4 5 6 7 8 9 10 11 12 13 14 15 16 17 18 19 20 21 22 23 24 25 26 27 28 29 30 31

AFROTEC MOVES WITH NIGERIA   AGENTS FOR RayGo

Art direction

for another. However this attitude is far from being representative of agencies as a whole. Some of the most creative and visually exciting photographic solutions to advertising problems can now be seen on hoardings in all parts of the world.

There are two basic approaches to the advertising photograph, each requiring a different degree of direct control on the part of the art director. The first could be termed 'illustrative/representational', implying a faithful and technically perfect rendering of some specific object, such as a pack, where the creative input on the part of the photographer is directed towards technical excellence rather than visual flair. In this case, the art director needs to exercise fairly rigid control, as the responsibility for the final advertisement will probably be his alone. However, in the case of a basic 'pack shot', photography allows for considerable scope in how the product will finally appear. A hen's egg, for example, can be lit and scaled in such a way as to make it appear eighteen inches tall and made of solid gold. By the same token, very ordinary sausages can be invested with qualities that render them far more desirable than when seen in the flesh, so to speak. It is this dilemma which is at the centre of the moral issues which surround advertising, and the designer needs to be aware of his responsibilities, not only to his employer and to his client, but also to society as a whole.

A different situation arises when the photograph has to be 'pictorial/situational' thereby calling for the maximum creative input on the part of the photographer in translating the art director's basic brief; this to some extent reverses the creative roles of the two protagonists, so that the art director is in the passive role of a user of the photographer's creative work, rather than his technical skills. In this

Theatre poster produced by a combination of a line derivative photoprint, an engraving and a flat cut-out image.

Art direction

case, the art director must at all costs avoid assuming a dictatorial attitude. The photographer will have been chosen for his particular talent for, say, creating atmosphere or characterization and must be allowed to pursue it in his own way.

Illustration page 47   The composite photograph by Jon Harris, used to advertise an expensive watch, is an example of how art direction and photography can combine to apply aesthetic ideals to a medium which only too often demands simple banality.

Art directing photography requires two basic skills – an understanding of what can be achieved on the technical level and an ability to explain exactly what is required to the photographer. When a purely photographic solution is required by the designer, the result will only be as good as the photographer and the ability of the designer to art direct him.

Illustration page 44   The design for a poster for Haig Whisky started life as a pencil rough on an envelope. Prior to any exposure to the client, the idea was discussed at some length with the photographer in order to ascertain how various effects could best be achieved. It is only at this point that a convincing finished rough can be produced. The final shot was therefore a straightforward affair, most of the art directing having been previously accomplished.

Illustration page 51   The photographs for a furniture brochure, on the other hand, demanded continuous supervision and collaboration with the photographer, because the basic ideas, although comparatively simple to plan in a general sense, could only be finalized in the studio.

The intention was to produce a comparatively low cost brochure whilst injecting a degree of interest over and above the products themselves. This was achieved by the slightly surrealistic approach of

The Overground Theatre
Clarence St, Kingston (opp Kingston station)
Box office 549 5893

Tambourine Man
An impression of Bob Dylan
by Tony Heywood and Leigh Jackson
Thurs Dec 4-Sun Dec 7
Wed Dec 10-Sun Dec 14
8pm, Admission £1
includes coffee and biscuits

Theatre poster using mixed media collage.

Art direction
Image manipulation

implying human involvement without actually using models – the impression of someone having just vacated the various environments was created in a variety of ways – a rocking chair still rocking, ink spilled from a desk, an 'out of frame' telephone call. The cost savings on photography, in addition to not using models, were achieved by creating an atmosphere through the use of props alone: walls, floors and ceilings were implied by lighting a paper back-drop curved from the vertical to the horizontal.

Illustration page 53   The requirement for the cover of a toy racing car catalogue was to create as much of an impression of reality as possible without resorting to the use of real cars. No attempt was made to simulate environment – rather, all emphasis was put on the idea of speed. The background was simply a scoop of coloured paper, lit in such a way as to lose the vertical. The cars were static, the impression of movement and speed being created by carefully applying Vaseline to a filter on the camera lens. The designer needs to know what is possible and what is not before embarking on what can prove to be extremely expensive experiments.

Image manipulation   The depth of focus on a process camera is sufficient to cope with flat original artwork that is moderately undulated or angled on the copy

Illustration page 55   board in order to distort images. The Wigmore Hall symbol, for example, was produced by drawing five parallel lines on a sheet of paper and undulating the paper under the projector. In a similar way, the Globe Playhouse flag, the EFTA and the Jubilee Tourist Centre symbols were drawn flat and the original distorted. Too steep a distortion produces a blurred effect, which can be turned to

Illustration page 57   advantage; all versions of the word 'typography' were photographed on the projector using ordinary document copying paper for the prints.

*Brochure covers combining
drawing and line photographs.*

Image manipulation

However useful and versatile a process camera set-up may be, a fully equipped photographic darkroom is obviously preferable, but it requires considerably more knowledge and skill to use to full advantage. A photographic enlarger has an almost limitless range of possibilities for image-manipulation, because the image is projected by throwing light through a negative (instead of reflected light being thrown from a positive). Double prints can be produced by sandwiching two negatives together, or alternatively two enlargers can be used to throw the images on to the same sheet of paper simultaneously, as with the coins on a brochure spread for a financial organisation. Solarization can be achieved by briefly exposing the printing paper to light during its development; areas of the projected image can be given prominence by masking out surrounding areas during exposure, either by specific objects, which will produce silhouettes on the final print, or by bits of card or paper; the photographic paper can be moved beneath the enlarger, producing either a blurred image or a multiple repeat image, or the paper can be tipped at an angle or undulated to produce distortions with a rather deeper field than a projector can manage.

There are several basic methods of achieving distortion effects apart from actually distorting the original under a process camera or

Illustration page 61 enlarger. One is the use of a distortion camera, consisting of a series of 'bent' lenses, arranged in such a way within the camera casing as to produce two or three distortion effects at once. For example, the artwork can be stretched horizontally and tipped in perspective vertically, the combined result appearing on one negative. As these contraptions are expensive, it would be uneconomical for an individual designer to invest in one, but there are various firms who

Festival of the City of London
17–28 July 1978
Artistic Director: Ian Hunter

Gilbert & Sullivan's   Symphony Orchestras
'Yeomen of the Guard' Choral Concerts
in   Recitals
the moat of the   Operas
Tower of London   in
Performances   St Paul's Cathedral
17 July–12 August   Southwark Cathedral
Fun for all!!!   Mansion House
Full supporting   Guildhall
Carnival programme   City Livery Halls & Churches

Full details:
Festival Box Office, St Paul's Churchyard, London EC4
Telephone: 01-248 8465 Monday–Friday 10am–6pm
and from all branches of Keith Prowse

Brighton Festival
28 April – 7 May 1978
Artistic Director: Ian Hunter

Tickets from:
29 New Road, Brighton, Sussex
BN1 1UG / Tel: 682127
Concerts · Exhibitions   Information from:
Opera · Entertainment   Marlborough House, Old Steine,
Films · Theatre   Brighton, Sussex BN1 1EQ / Tel: 29801

Malvern Festival
22 May – 11 June 1978

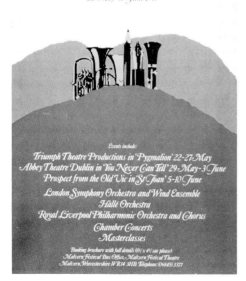

Events include:
Triumph Theatre Productions in 'Pygmalion' 22–27 May
Abbey Theatre Dublin in 'You Never Can Tell' 29 May–3 June
Prospect from the Old Vic in 'St Joan' 5–10 June
London Symphony Orchestra and Wind Ensemble
Hallé Orchestra
Royal Liverpool Philharmonic Orchestra and Chorus
Chamber Concerts
Masterclasses

Booking brochure with full details (8½ x 4½ sae please)
Malvern Festival Box Office, Malvern Festival Theatre
Malvern, Worcestershire WR14 3HB Telephone: 06845 3377

Brighton Festival
2–17 May 1981
Artistic Director: Ian Hunter

including
Moscow Philharmonic
Philharmonia · Concertgebouw
London Symphony Orchestra
Scottish Ballet · Bubble Theatre
New Sussex Opera
Exhibition:
'Eat, Drink and be Merry'

Full Festival Details:
Festival Office,
Marlborough House,
Old Steine, Brighton
Telephone (0273) 29801 x 8121

Arts Festival posters using a variety of mixed media techniques – drawing, cut paper, photo collage and film overlays.

specialize in providing this service. The problem for the designer in this case is how to specify the exact effect required. To a large extent, the most interesting results are achieved through trial and error, and it is advisable for the designer to persuade the camera operator to allow him to be present while the effect is being set up, and dictate whatever adjustments need to be made.

Illustration page 63   An alternative method employs a conventional camera, a lightbox, and optical overlay units. The units consist of various distorting 'lenses' which are placed over film positives or negatives on the lightbox. The image is then photographed conventionally. If two distorting effects are required on the same original, the result from the first overlay-unit must be rephotographed, using a second unit. This method has the advantage that the designer can control precisely the result he requires, but it is somewhat more laborious than using a distorting camera.

The method of image distortion which probably holds the most possibilities is the projection of slides on to shaped or naturally distorted surfaces and rephotographing with a conventional camera. The obvious advantage is that almost any surface from a nude figure to a teapot can be used. One of the most memorable examples of this technique was Robert Brownjohn's title sequence for the James Bond *Goldfinger* film, where moving typography was projected on to a girl's body painted gold.

Animation
Illustration page 65   Some extreme (but simple) distortion effects can be achieved 'in the camera', providing the lens has sufficient focal depth. The stills from an animated title-sequence were for a BBC television play. When the film is run, the bulls appear to turn through 180 degrees. Artwork for this was prepared by mounting reversed black-to-white photoprints of

Theatre poster depicting the principal actor – a portrait photograph being the only available reference.

Animation

the bulls (from engravings by Bewick) on to board, and using a
10×8in. (203×254mm) plate camera, photographing them first of all
square on to the lens, then turned by 15 degrees, then 30 degrees and
so on until they disappeared, eventually being at right angles to the
camera. The process was then repeated, using reversed left-to-right
prints. The final distorted prints were then filmed consecutively
exposing three frames per print with a two-frame dissolve between
each. Although this method may seem cumbersome to achieve a
comparatively simple movement, it is in fact easier to control than
filming the prints in live action while they turn. For example, the
edge of the card, when turned at a steep angle to the movie camera,
would almost certainly show up on the film and the background
would be difficult to match exactly. Using consecutive stills, all
'foreign bodies' can be painted out on the negative before final prints
are made for filming.

Title sequences for film or television represent a fascinating area for
the graphic designer, who is more often than not brought up on a diet
of static images. The basic principals are simple, and a great deal of
movement and tension can be created by illusion rather than
laborious animation.

A simple rostrum camera working over flat artwork can achieve
four basic movements; pull in and out and pan sideways or vertically.
Further effects and movements can be achieved by manipulating the
artwork under the camera.

Illustration page 67 Due to certain logistical problems experienced by the production
company, the opening and closing sequences for *Wolcott* had to be
conceived, artworked and shot within a week. Obviously there was no
possibility for any complex technical wizardry; the solution had to be

A photograph reproduced from a magazine and an 8×enlargement.

Animation

technically straightforward, but at the same time reflect the violent and fast moving action of the film. The opening sequence was constructed from two basic images; the main character and a shotgun. The actor was photographed in a single position, multiple line prints being made from the original continuous tone print.

Due to a sub-plot concerning the ambiguous racial situation in which a black policeman found himself in a dominantly white environment, the prints were reversed black to white for the first section.

The action starts when the viewer moves along the line of identical figures. This is achieved by moving the artwork beneath the fixed lens of the rostrum camera by equal amounts for each exposure. There are 25 frames per second at normal projection speed; therefore, if three seconds' movement time is required, the total distance of movement must be divided by 75; (i.e. 75 separate movements). It is possible to expose two frames per movement, thereby cutting down the rostrum work, but a less smooth effect will be produced.

The next action involves the viewer stopping, and from the centre one of the figures moves forward into full close-up. Because the background figures must remain static whilst the foreground figure enlarges, the camera lens cannot move in on the artwork. Multiple prints of the foreground figure must therefore be prepared on overlays, each one slightly larger than the last, and dissolved into one another until the final shot is arrived at. Dissolves are achieved by exposing the static artwork while simultaneously stopping *down* the camera frame by frame until no image is registered. The camera is then rewound to the first stopped down frame, and the new artwork exposed by the same number of frames whilst simultaneously

Hicks into the 80's

Brochure cover combining two full colour photographs.

stopping *up* to full image exposure.

Following the apparent zoom in, the close-up dissolves from negative to positive while the first title appears. The simplest way to achieve this is to prepare the typography on transparent film overlays which can be positioned exactly over the existing image. However, a blank sheet of the transparent material must be used over all previous images in the same sequence, as the slight change in tonal quality produced by shooting through acetate is noticeable.

The title then dissolves into a gun barrel which slowly swings round until facing the viewer. Again, a series of dissolves based on a series of previously taken photographs.

The gun explodes into blood, finally enveloping the screen in solid red. This is achieved simply by working directly under the camera with red paint, spreading the splash frame by frame.

The end sequence follows a similar pattern (black and white chess pieces being used as an analogy) where the illusion of movement is created by continuous dissolves of previously prepared artwork.

Illustration page 69   Though the techniques employed in the production of the *Very Like A Whale* sequence were similar (i.e. simple movements of artwork beneath the camera coupled with dissolves) one additional and very simple technique was employed.

The rose image was required to slowly 'bleed' of its colour; this was achieved by preparing the basic image on photographic film rather than paper, the image itself being transparent. Colour was added with a sheet of Pantone paper behind the film which was withdrawn, frame by frame, until only a white background remained.

Photo-collage   Photo-collage has been in use since the invention of photography. There are many instances of its use by artists from Picasso to Warhol,

Illustration for a comedy spy story.

Photo-collage

Illustration page 71 not forgetting perhaps its most important exponent, John Heartfield, whose 'photo comments' on Germany's 1930s war ambitions must rank amongst the most committed examples of graphic art of this century.

Since the upsurge of interest amongst graphic designers in the work of Magritte and, for that matter Heartfield, the surrealistic possibilities inherent in photo-collage are being fully exploited, especially by Polish poster designers. The basic tensions which exist between reality and unreality can be both riveting and persuasive, and the photograph used in conjunction with stylized drawing techniques is an ideal graphic combination to express this. In almost every field of graphics, photo-collage techniques are employed in one form or another: posters, animated films, fashion magazine spreads, book jackets, even trademarks.

Illustration page 73 The cover for a pension fund leaflet combines a flat drawn shape with a cut-out photographic treatment of hallmarks. The idea, though different in essence, could have been reversed to equal effect, i.e. the hallmarks could have been drawn on to a real egg and a photograph taken of the result. In either event, the image is perhaps more interesting than if completely drawn or photographed.

Equally effective use of counterpoint can be achieved by mixing two or more phototechniques together. Illustration page 75 The pages for a calendar for a Nigerian heavy equipment supplier combine line derivative images with full colour cut-out photographs. To some extent this was the result of *force majeure*; the only available reference for the firm's products were black and white photographs of dubious and varying quality; some kind of reduction technique was therefore necessary to sharpen the images into a consistent quality. Full colour studio shots

Cover and spreads from a company magazine employing a variety of photo-techniques.

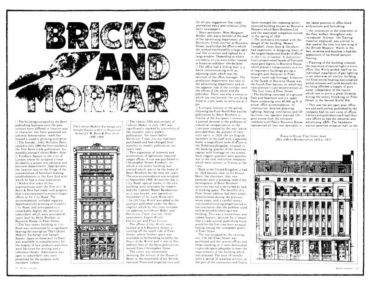

BRICKS AND MORTAR

The Lure of Leather

Miracles
by C. G. Drummond

Photo-collage
Scale

of the two girls were taken with a 5×4in camera, the advantage of this apparatus being that it has a ground viewing screen onto which the image is thrown, enabling a small layout showing the machine positions to be inserted; the photographer is therefore able to position the models exactly to the layouts.

Illustration page 77 Bizarre effects can easily be achieved by marrying up images which normally do not relate. The somewhat eerie atmostphere of *The Trouble With Ants* poster is due in part to the larger-than-life eyes of the astronaut (taken from a nineteenth-century engraving) while the main image is a line derivative photograph. The ant is a cut-paper collage. There was no attempt here to produce a realistic image as the situation is obviously ridiculous.

Illustration page 79 The poster for *Tambourine Man* similarly mixes cut-paper collage with a photoprint from an engraving, although in this instance the
Illustration page 81 engraving was 'smashed' with a pair of scissors. The car hire brochure
Illustration page 83 covers mix drawings with line photographs, as do the four arts festival posters.

Illustration page 85 The poster for Shakespeare's play *Timon of Athens* (another design for the same play is shown elsewhere in this book), although apparently simple, involved a relatively complicated series of photo-collage steps in order to arrive at the final stage.

The foreground figure is a compilation of line derivatives taken from a studio shot (robed body and hands), a theatre publicity photograph (the head), and part of an indian fabric design (the necklace). The background figures are a collage of photocopies taken from magazines and re-touched. A flat dot screen was used over the robe in order to avoid printing a third colour.

Scale Quite ordinary things can be invested with a visual drama, or

Magazine spreads integrating image and typography.

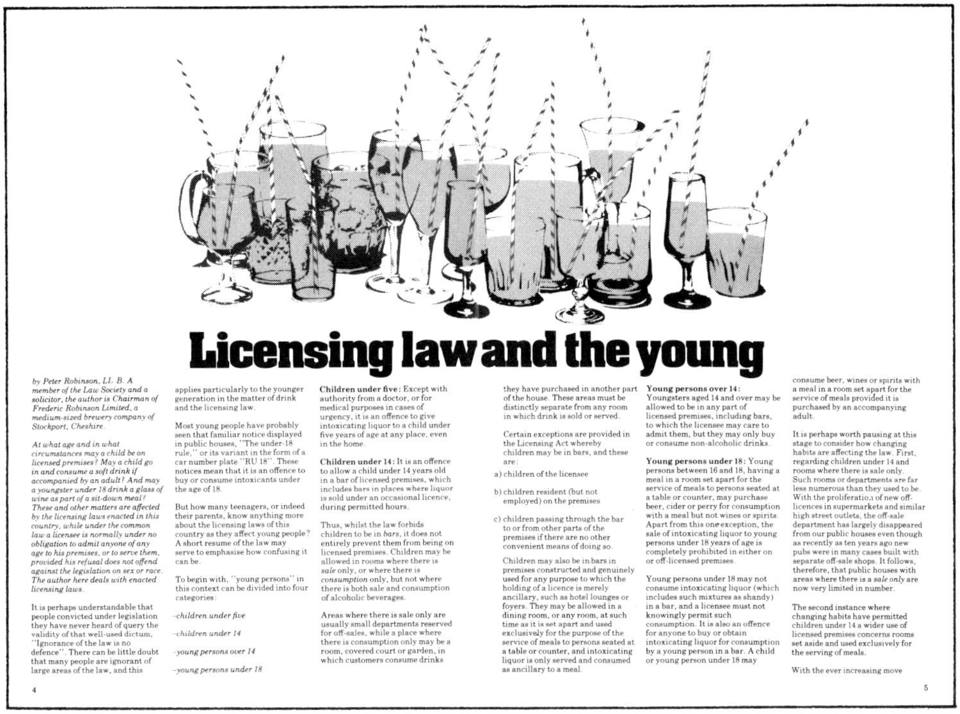

Licensing law and the young

by Peter Robinson, Ll. B. A member of the Law Society and a solicitor, the author is Chairman of Frederic Robinson Limited, a medium-sized brewery company of Stockport, Cheshire.

At what age and in what circumstances may a child be on licensed premises? May a child go in and consume a soft drink if accompanied by an adult? And may a youngster under 18 drink a glass of wine as part of a sit-down meal? These and other matters are affected by the licensing laws enacted in this country, while under the common law a licensee is normally under no obligation to admit anyone of any age to his premises, or to serve them, provided his refusal does not offend against the legislation on sex or race. The author here deals with enacted licensing laws.

It is perhaps understandable that people convicted under legislation they have never heard of query the validity of that well-used dictum, "Ignorance of the law is no defence". There can be little doubt that many people are ignorant of large areas of the law, and this applies particularly to the younger generation in the matter of drink and the licensing law.

Most young people have probably seen that familiar notice displayed in public houses, "The under-18 rule," or its variant in the form of a car number plate "RU 18". These notices mean that it is an offence to buy or consume intoxicants under the age of 18.

But how many teenagers, or indeed their parents, know anything more about the licensing laws of this country as they affect young people? A short resume of the law may serve to emphasise how confusing it can be.

To begin with, "young persons" in this context can be divided into four categories:

-*children under five*

-*children under 14*

-*young persons over 14*

-*young persons under 18*

Children under five: Except with authority from a doctor, or for medical purposes in cases of urgency, it is an offence to give intoxicating liquor to a child under five years of age at any place, even in the home.

Children under 14: It is an offence to allow a child under 14 years old in a bar of licensed premises, which includes bars in places where liquor is sold under an occasional licence, during permitted hours.

Thus, whilst the law forbids children to be in *bars*, it does not entirely prevent them from being on licensed premises. Children may be allowed in rooms where there is *sale* only, or where there is *consumption* only, but not where there is both sale and consumption of alcoholic beverages.

Areas where there is sale only are usually small departments reserved for off-sales, while a place where there is consumption only may be a room, covered court or garden, in which customers consume drinks they have purchased in another part of the house. These areas must be distinctly separate from any room in which drink is sold or served.

Certain exceptions are provided in the Licensing Act whereby children may be in bars, and these are:

a) children of the licensee

b) children resident (but not employed) on the premises

c) children passing through the bar to or from other parts of the premises if there are no other convenient means of doing so.

Children may also be in bars in premises constructed and genuinely used for any purpose to which the holding of a licence is merely ancillary, such as hotel lounges or foyers. They may be allowed in a dining room, or any room, at such time as it is set apart and used exclusively for the purpose of the service of meals to persons seated at a table or counter, and intoxicating liquor is only served and consumed as ancillary to a meal.

Young persons over 14: Youngsters aged 14 and over may be allowed to be in any part of licensed premises, including bars, to which the licensee may care to admit them, but they may only buy or consume non-alcoholic drinks.

Young persons under 18: Young persons between 16 and 18, having a meal in a room set apart for the service of meals to persons seated at a table or counter, may purchase beer, cider or perry for consumption with a meal but not wines or spirits. Apart from this one exception, the sale of intoxicating liquor to young persons under 18 years of age is completely prohibited in either on or off-licensed premises.

Young persons under 18 may not consume intoxicating liquor (which includes such mixtures as shandy) in a bar, and a licensee must not knowingly permit such consumption. It is also an offence for anyone to buy or obtain intoxicating liquor for consumption by a young person in a bar. A child or young person under 18 may consume beer, wines or spirits with a meal in a room set apart for the service of meals provided it is purchased by an accompanying adult.

It is perhaps worth pausing at this stage to consider how changing habits are affecting the law. First, regarding children under 14 and rooms where there is sale only. Such rooms or departments are far less numerous than they used to be. With the proliferation of new off-licences in supermarkets and similar high street outlets, the off-sale department has largely disappeared from our public houses even though as recently as ten years ago new pubs were in many cases built with separate off-sale shops. It follows, therefore, that public houses with areas where there is a *sale only* are now very limited in number.

The second instance where changing habits have permitted children under 14 a wider use of licensed premises concerns rooms set aside and used exclusively for the serving of meals.

With the ever increasing move

4

5

THE DRINK PROBLEM IN INDUSTRY

By Allan F. Blacklaws, Managing Director, Group Services, Scottish and Newcastle Breweries, Ltd. Mr Blacklaws is a Fellow of the British Institute of Management, Companion of the Institute of Personnel Management and Chairman of the Industrial Relations Committee of the Brewers' Association of Scotland.

People may argue about the causes of problem drinking and whether it is an illness or a syndrome. They may disagree about what is really meant by problem drinking but one thing is not in dispute, and that is that the problem exists. Reports suggest it is becoming increasingly evident in the work place, despite attempts at concealment which take place, often for the best of reasons.

It is extremely difficult to measure the cost to industry in terms of poor work output or damage to industrial relations. Estimates of loss are necessarily subjective but there is no doubt they are very considerable indeed.

Likewise, it is impossible to prove if there is more or less abuse of alcohol today than in the early 1900s. The evidence of recent years, however, points to an increase in the problem, though to some extent the statistics reflect better reporting procedures and greater awareness of alcohol abuse.

Recognising the condition is always the first step in any remedial activity, and there has to be doubt about the extent to which this is currently achieved with any degree of skill in the industrial context. This is the experience of one manager:

"At first when he admitted he was an alcoholic I was very surprised. I knew he had been a fairly heavy drinker for years and on occasion arrived home very drunk in the wee sma' 'oors. But an alcoholic? Impossible!

"Then I recalled a number of incidents – apparently innocent at the time. I realised that recently his work had deteriorated. Deadlines had been missed; errors were common and careless mistakes, which could not easily be explained, were being made. On many occasions he had been off as a result of an 'upset stomach' or he was 'not feeling well' or 'the car wouldn't start' or 'the dog ran away'. I wonder now how I could have missed all these signs. Yet as they occurred none of these incidents seemed to be interrelated."

For us and industry generally, the problem of identifying the potential excessive drinker is the crux of the matter. If real progress is to be made, firm preventive and curative steps need to be taken, and this is what we in Scottish and Newcastle Breweries faced up to about three years ago.

Some of the truths we has to recognise were, first, that alcoholism contributes to the mortality rate in Scotland to a greater extent than all other causes except heart disease and cancer. Second, it appears that employees in the drinks industry are amongst the high risk categories. Third, the people involved include not only manual workers but also salaried staff right up to senior executive and director levels.

Against this background we decided on a positive line and our policy began to emerge in discussion with the Scottish Health Education Unit and the Scottish Council on Alcoholism.

If employers have been slow to respond to the growing need to develop an educational, preventative and corrective course of action on problem drinking, then this is probably no less true of the trade union movement. Among its welfare benefits for members, aid for the casualties of alcohol misuse is negligible.

We recognised that an alcoholism policy would need the positive support of the trade unions. Quite apart from problem drinking which requires remedial action, managers have disciplinary issues to deal with and unions have a vital interest in these. Not only did we recognise the essential need to carry the trade unions with us, and especially the shop floor representatives, but also we had to accept that the role of managers and shop stewards was similar, namely to identify behavioural patterns in the context of work performance.

Policies are worthless without corresponding practices; and we accepted the reality of the cloak of secrecy and concealment which surrounded alcohol related problems. We had to consider how to act sensitively while making some tentative steps forward. How was this to be done?

If insecurity is a symptom and arguably a cause of problem drinking, then this was clearly one area where we as an employer could help. Supportive family relationships are enormously important in remedial treatment, but the significance of secure employment cannot be underestimated. Security of employment is the basic company guarantee to employees undergoing treatment.

The problems of discipline remained, especially in dealing with border line cases. It was one thing to take positive steps to deal with a major problem but quite another to regard every 'morning after the night before' as a sudden attack of alcoholism. Clearly a behavioural pattern had to be established, but more than that, some commitment to corrective treatment was required from the individuals themselves.

On the basis of considerations of this kind we consulted the full-time officials of our trade unions on a draft policy. Agreement was not difficult to reach and on reflection we found this not surprising. From the union point of view it gave added security of employment to some of their members who were 'sick', while in the disciplinary sense very little was changed. We found there was a genuine desire on the part of union officials and shop stewards to come to grips with a problem which they knew to exist. They were anxious to co-operate and responded well to our lead.

Our policy can be stated in the following way:

* The Company recognises, from the nature of its business, that employees can be exposed to greater risks on problem drinking than in industry generally.

* It also acknowledges that alcoholism is an illness characterised by dependence on alcohol, either psychological or physical, or a combination of both. In the industrial context, it is defined as drinking which continually or repeatedly affects an employee's work performance.

* The most important signs of this can normally be detected by managers as:
- frequent lateness
- repeated brief periods of absence
- minor accidents on the job
- drinking at work
- changes of mood
- borrowing money
- lowering quality of work
- reduced quantity of output

Medical certificates for absence will frequently include diagnoses like gastro-enteritis, dyspepsia, nervous debility and so on.

* On recognition of a problem or potential problem, the manager will seek the advice of the personnel and medical departments who have the necessary professional contacts to start the treatment process.

* The individual will be encouraged to seek help and treatment on the understanding that:
i. He or she whilst undergoing treatment is considered to be on sick leave and will be entitled to the normal benefits from the company sickness benefit scheme.

ii. The company assures the employee concerned that his/her present position will be available upon return to work following treatment, unless it is mutually agreed that a change would be desirable and beneficial.

iii. No disciplinary action will be taken against the employee unless it is clear that the individual is incapable of responding to treatment or refuses the advice and guidance which has been given by the professional advisors invited to deal with the case.

iv. Any individual who claims that he/she does not require treatment will be warned under the normal disciplinary code concerned with behaviour and work performance.

* This policy is applicable to all employees from directors to wage

10

11

Scale

indeed their entire character can be changed by a manipulation of scale. However, the effect of scale is only relative to environment. A photograph of a man standing in front of a tree, if printed in a book of this size would appear to be perfectly ordinary, though his body would perhaps be only an inch or so high. If, however, the scale of his environment were manipulated by photo-collage so that he was only an inch high relative to the tree, then the effect would be surrealistic and grotesque.

Illustration page 87   The dot pattern is a blow-up of a section of a newspaper photograph. Because it is printed in a book, and therefore viewed closely, the dominant visual impact comes from the texture and pattern rather than from the subject matter (which becomes almost unrecognizable). If the same-size pattern were printed on a large advertising hoarding, it would turn back into the original image, and the subject matter would become the dominant factor.

Manipulation of scale is one of the more obvious advantages phototechniques can achieve. However, if this involves the marriage of two continuous tone photographs, great skill is required, especially when employing colour, if cut lines and 'stuck on' edges are to be avoided.

Illustration page 89   The brochure cover for an interior designer, 'Hicks into the '80s' was produced by two separate photographs being mixed into a single transparency. A model, about two feet high, was made of a three-dimensional version of his monogram. This was photographed against a matt black background (as was David Hicks himself) with careful lighting designed to emphasize form. A 5×4in. plate camera was used, firstly because distortion can be corrected, and secondly a large format is necessary to facilitate the difficult task of dropping one

Double page spreads from a book
designed by Massin.

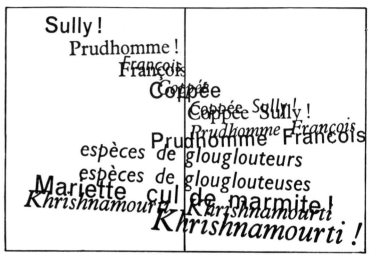

Scale
Photo-illustration
Phototype

colour image into another. In the event, a 10×8in. duplicate transparency was made from the original to assist the final artwork. This stage should be performed by a specialist company with the correct equipment and skills, as it is unlikely that it would be worthwhile for a design studio to employ such a facility.

Photo-illustration An area in which the use of phototechniques has so far failed to gain any strong foothold is fiction illustration. Superficially, the reason is obvious; photography traditionally deals with reality and its use in conjunction with imagined or ambiguous literary situations could prove to be too specific. However, if 'real' images are juxtaposed with obviously unreal elements, a fictional quality can be maintained. This

Illustration page 91 approach was used in the illustration (for a comedy spy book) to show the central character's bewilderment. The various official instructions at the top of the illustration have no specific presence, i.e. they are removed from their normal position on, say, the outside of a secret file. The man's bewilderment is therefore prompted by the conception of the instructions rather than their specific import. Illustratively, this is a basically fictional situation and the fact that a photograph was used for the man does not interfere with the fantasy of the total image.

Phototype For hundreds of years, in fact since the beginning of printing itself, typographers have been limited by the letterpress system of typesetting, along with all the rigidity that it implies. For example, type being cast on a body means that the special relationship of any given letter to another is strictly limited, i.e. it is impossible to *reduce* the space between letters further than the body on to which it is cast will allow. In instances such as a capital I following a capital A, the space between the letters will appear abnormally large in relation,

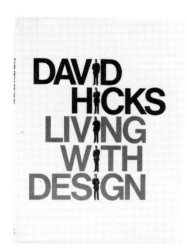

Book design exploiting pace and variety.

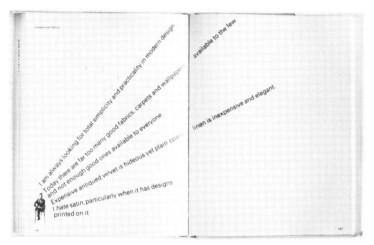

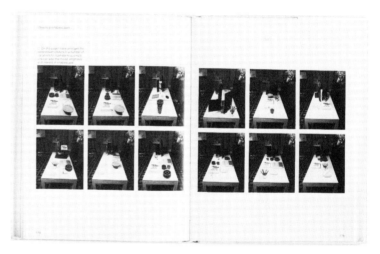

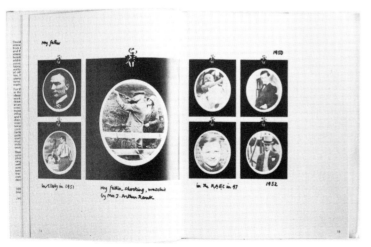

Phototype

say, to the space between a B and E. Some typefaces are certainly designed so as to minimize problems of legibility and appearance, but anomalies still occur.

However, with the advent of phototypesetting linked with a correctly programmed computer, these problems have been eliminated. Certain conclusions have been arrived at as a result of researches into legibility factors, such as ideal spacing between any given letters, optimum line lengths, and interlinear spacing for any given size of type, which can be programmed into a computer and translated on to film. (Metal typesetting, especially for letter spacing, has insufficient flexibility to cope with much sophisticated typography.)

The designer/typographer faces obvious difficulties in exploiting the potential inherent in the computer typesetting system, because he needs to be versed in the intricacies of computer programming, usually an alien discipline. Art schools and technical colleges, where most typographers are trained, have not generally tackled the problem in any depth, either because of lack of awareness of the potential, or lack of money with which to buy the computer.

Unfortunately most present day photosetting machines are operated in a similar way to conventional machines, i.e. by an operator typing out the copy on a keyboard. The setting itself is produced on film negative often with predetermined letter spacing as with lead setting, thereby showing no advance in terms of legibility or aesthetics. As a result, a fair proportion of photosetting turns out to be indistinguishable from metal setting when it appears on the printed page (or in some cases, worse).

With conventional metal typesetting, the larger the type the more

Symbol for a modern dance company; a collage of simplified photographic images.

masque

Phototype
Photo layout/magazines

glaring the spacing problems. For headlines, or any instances where type is to be larger than ordinary text, there are now photosetting machines which form a reasonable alternative to adhesive letter systems and are comparatively easy for the designer to use. They consist of either a disc or strip of film, with an alphabet negatived out of them, through which light is projected on to sensitized paper. They work in the same way as a conventional enlarger, so that an almost infinite variety of type size is available. It is also possible to fit a distorting lens on to the machine, which will italicize, condense or expand the basic alphabet. Letter spacing is infinitely controllable, simply by moving the sensitized paper between each letter exposure. As each letter is exposed separately, it is obviously impractical to set anything more than headlines, as text setting would be far too laborious; nevertheless, the system is as quick to use as self-adhesive type, and has a wider range of sizes.

Photo layout/magazines   The vast majority of pictorial representation in books, magazines and newspapers is photographic. Most advertising now relies on photographs for its images, as do packaging, public relations and information publications, book jackets, record sleeves, and so on. What has not been sufficiently realized during the period in which the photographic explosion has taken place, is that the effect of any given photograph depends to a great extent on its visual environment. The relationship between a photograph and the page on which it appears can make or destroy not only the impact of the photograph itself but the visual balance between it and other elements which appear in that environment, such as text, other photographs, drawings, etc.

In a magazine spread, for example, there should be several layers of comprehension on the part of the reader; the nature of the medium is

El Greco painting and a book jacket derived from it.

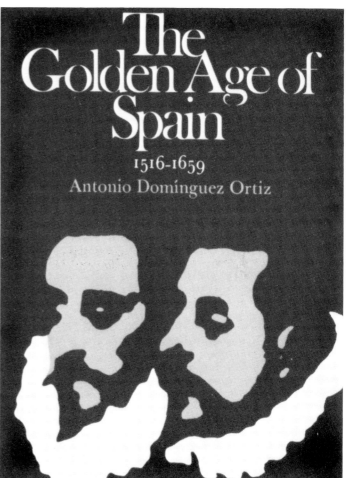

The
Golden Age of
Spain
1516-1659
Antonio Domínguez Ortiz

Photo layout/magazines

essentially ephemeral, and it should be possible to grasp the essence of a spread with a cursory glance, before being drawn into it on an emotional or intellectual level. There is, in this situation, a certain conflict which must be resolved by the designer. In order to produce an immediate sympathetic response, photographs and other visual material need to be used in such a way as to produce the maximum impact from their subject matter. At the same time, they must not be over-used, in the sense that their interest is 'used up' by the time the reader involves himself with the article; a reasonable balance must also be maintained between the visual and literary content. Naturally a great deal depends on the quality of the photographs themselves but, if badly used, their quality or relevance can be negated.

New dimensions can be added to photographic images simply by their juxtaposition. On a simple level, a photograph of an English corn field, when placed next to a picture of famine in Pakistan, carries quite different implications than if it were next to a picture of a loaf of bread.

Astute selection of only the relevant areas of an original photograph (cropping) can play a large part in focusing attention on its salient visual factors. This is something which obviously needs to be practised with great care – photographers can often react violently when their original artwork is mutilated, and frequently with reason. On a less obvious level, the purely abstract arrangement of pictures and type on a page can carry with it a certain communicative atmosphere. A strict grid Mondrian-type layout with well-balanced tonal distribution would imply a sense of order and responsibility which would be suited to say, a company report, or an article on town planning, but would probably not stimulate a sympathetic response if

*Image from a poster produced by
repeated photocopying of a
continuous tone photograph.*

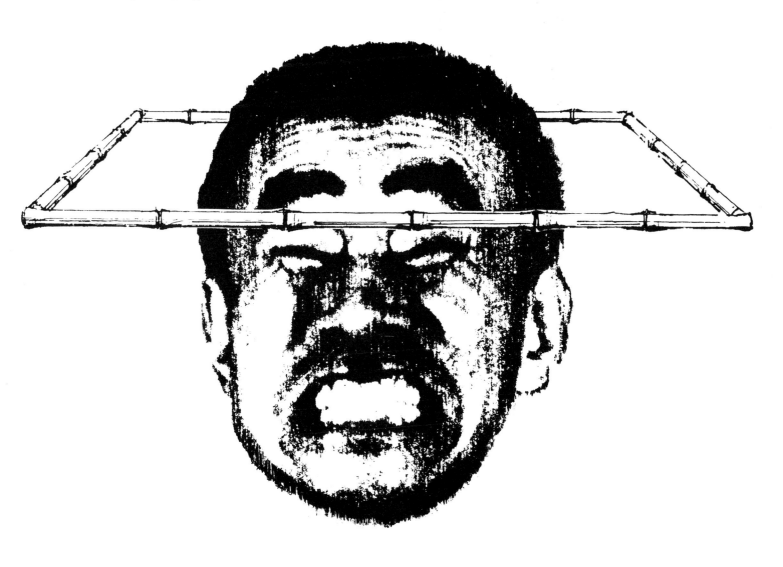

Photo layout/magazines
Photo layout/books

applied to an article on pop groups.

The designer or art director is in a position to control at least the initial response to a page, though he may not leave a lasting impression after its contents have been wholly ingested. The responsibility of the designer, especially in magazine work, is therefore initially to involve the reader and to reflect accurately the editorial intention.

Magazines offer enormous scope to the designer for the use of phototechniques. The *Benn Centenary* magazine, a one-off publication dealing with various and very diverse aspects of a publisher's output, lent itself particularly to exploiting many different approaches.

The cover, implying a hundred years' output, is a composite of two photographs: one of the covers of some current publications, the other an end-on shot of some magazines of which twenty prints were made and pasted together to create the illusion of quantity. If the end result were to have been produced by a single photograph, over three thousand magazines would have been required, with all the setting-up problems which that implies.

The spread entitled 'Miracles', an article about dubious or quack medical cures in the nineteenth century, has an image produced by marrying differently sized photoprints taken from old catalogues.

The 'Bricks and Mortar' page incorporates a cut-out half tone, the impression of reality being heightened by the inclusion of a shadow.

The 'Lure of Leather' spread is a collage of line derivative prints taken from separate continuous tone photographs.

The spreads from a journal for the Brewers' Society utilize a combination of photoprints, drawing and flat screen overlays.

Photo layout/books In book design the problems for the designer are somewhat

Illustration page 93

Illustration page 95

Theatre poster; artwork produced on a simple photocopying machine.

STRIKE STRIKE STRIKE STRIKE STRIKE!

THE MATCHGIRLS

A musical
by Bill Owen and Tony Russell
at Group 64 Theatre
203b Upper Richmond Road, SW15
from
March 7th — 12th
Tickets 50p Monday/Tuesday
65p Wednesday/Thursday/Friday/
Saturday
Available from the theatre
(Tel: 788 6943)
or Cobb and Webb, Putney

Photo layout/books

different, the book being a less ephemeral medium than magazines. In the last fifteen years or so, there has been an ever-increasing stream of books which are mainly photographic, using text more as a support to the picture than as the central content of the book. The label 'coffee table book' is perhaps misleading, in the sense that it implies a lack of seriousness in the work, but basically this category of publications has been a big factor in the fortunes of some publishers. In quality they have ranged from glossy productions with little or no content, to serious, well-presented books of scholarship. The role of the designer in this field is crucial; generally speaking, he is less concerned with initial impact (except for the cover) than in magazines, but rather more involved in the coherence and flow of the content, whilst synthesizing the material into an integrated totality. Without the designer or 'chef', a collection of photographs, however intrinsically good they may be individually, can become meaningless as a sequential narrative if presented arbitrarily. If the nature of the book is primarily visual, then the editorial direction must be elucidated by visual means. Unfortunately, many books have been produced in the past with no thought given to this problem, and it has often been deemed adequate to dispense with the services of a designer and hang a few full colour pictures together with a title and some captions – hence the slightly dubious connotations of the description 'coffee table'.

However, there is a positive side, often producing exciting results. Illustration page 97 For example the designer Massin, working in France, has designed several books using highly literate texts, and with the use of photography and phototechniques such as maximum contrast treatments, distortion, overprinting, etc., has evolved a kind of visual

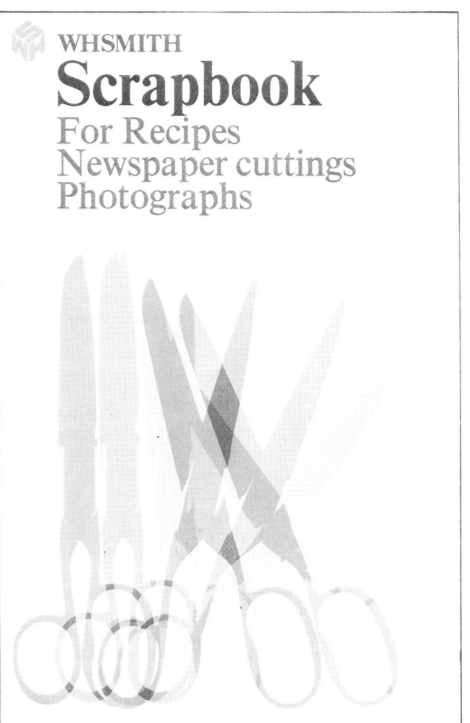

Scissor image produced by overlaying photocopies of the actual object in different positions.

Photo layout/books

experience not unlike watching a play being performed. The illustrations here show spreads from *La Cantratrice Chauve* by Ionesco. In this instance, the designer becomes a kind of producer, or co-author. This is perhaps an extreme example of designer participation, but certainly none the less valid for that.

On a more restrained level, involving straight photographs and text, the designer needs to have some understanding of, and sympathy with, his material. Photographs, if they are good, will express something which must not be negated by the designer treating them as abstract pattern on a page, while disregarding the content or mood of the material.

Illustration page 99 Picture books in particular, should be an experience with pace, rhythm, surprise and style. The text for the book on David Hicks was produced by taping a series of interviews, usually in the environment under discussion, while the relevant rooms or details were photographed. In addition, visual material came from archives, press cuttings, drawings, or simply fabric or wallpaper samples.

The layout througout the book deliberately avoids any set grid system, allowing every spread a freedom of design relevant to its subject. This was possible due to the art direction of the photography and editorial control being vested in the designer, allowing each spread to be conceived as a separate, though integrated, entity. The book can therefore be read from back to front or simply dipped into at any point. This somewhat unconventional approach is far from suited to most books, but in this case it seemed apposite as the book was dealing with many attitudes and facets of a single person's work.

The cover was produced by substituting full colour cut-out photographs of David Hicks for the 'I' in the title. Designers can often

Photo-silk screen images fired onto ceramic mugs.

be blessed with good fortune. A title with an 'I' in every word is a good start and by arranging the figures one above the other, the resultant typography works satisfactorily in its own right. The trick is simply to perceive the possibilities in the first place.

Realism

Illustration page 101

The special quality that photography can lend to an image, however changed or distorted it may become in the designer's hands, is one of reality. The Masque dance troupe symbol, though mostly drawn is based on photographs. The artwork started as maximum contrast photoprints which were then simplified, and to some extent abstracted.

Illustration page 103

A phototechnique such as this can be taken to the extreme in turning an illustration back into a basically photographic image. The book jacket for *The Golden Age of Spain* is in fact a small section of an El Greco painting, rephotographed from a black-and-white reproduction on to line film (hard contrast) and the surrounding details painted out on the negative; the flat colour was then printed into the faces, leaving the ruffles white. The reasoning behind this is that the El Greco heads seemed to express exactly the period and character of the book, but if reproduced 'straight', would have lacked impact on what is basically a selling package, competing for attraction with literally hundreds of other jackets in a bookshop. By abstracting the image into hard areas of colour and tone, a more compelling graphic image is produced. This is not to say that the process has added anything to the original, quite the reverse. It has just adapted it to the specific requirements of the medium in which it is used. There may, however, be some moral objections to this attitude, but I suspect that El Greco himself would not have minded too much.

W H Smith & Son (Holdings) Limited and Subsidiary Companies
Ten year record, profit before tax

Full colour cut out photograph used in a company report.

£9,860,000

£6,518,000

£4,689,000

£4,068,000
£3,834,000

£3,049,000
£2,753,000
£2,622,000
£2,577,000
£2,488,000

63/64 64/65 65/66 66/67 67/68 68/69 69/70 70/71 71/72 72/73

20

Photocopies
Scope

Photocopies Ordinary dry process photocopy machines can be used to great advantage in the production of a wide range of images. It is important, though, that they should have the facility to copy onto a variety of papers.

Illustration page 105 The portrait of a Japanese dancer, used on a poster to publicize his performances, was the result of a technique developed to mitigate the poor quality of the only available original. A straightforward photocopy was made from a continuous tone print. This was worked on with process white paint and black ink in order to eliminate unwanted areas and highlight others. This was in turn re-copied, re-worked on, and finally re-copied, the last print being moved slightly during exposure to produce a degree of vertical grain. The bamboo surround, symbolizing psychological imprisonment, was added by overlaying a cut-out drawing.

Most modern copiers can produce an image of sufficient quality to be used directly as artwork, so long as tone gradations are not required.

Illustration page 107 The poster for *The Matchgirls*, for example, was produced by a collage of photocopies from a book of engravings with the addition of flat colour areas.

Illustration page 109 The cover for a scrapbook using a pair of scissors in various positions was achieved by overlaying a series of photocopies of the object itself and printing each layer in a different transluscent colour.

Scope The designer who has some knowledge and command of phototechniques not only widens his scope in terms of visual treatments, but also enlarges the areas of operation open to him. The graphic use of photography need not be limited to flat paper surfaces. Textiles, plastics, ceramics, etc., all traditionally rely on drawn images for their decoration and could all benefit from some new

Two simple images constructed
from photo-copies.

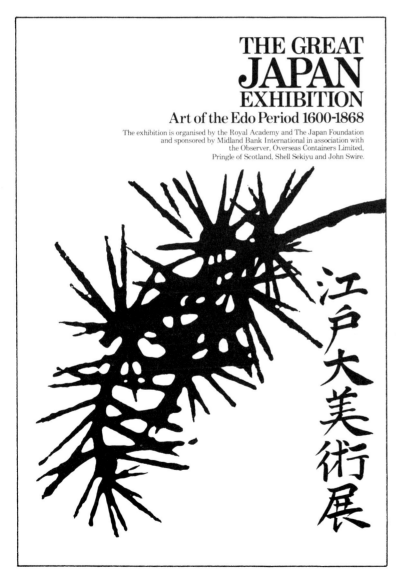

design techniques.

The designs shown on mugs are fired ceramic transfers, silk-screen printed in red and orange. The original continuous tone photograph was taken to line and a solid area tracing was made from the print. This was printed down first, as an orange silhouette, the red detailing being overprinted to fit. Ceramic-transfer silk-screen colours have a particular luminosity when fired; without previous experience the exact colours are often unpredictable, but the depth of colour that can be achieved surpasses any conventional printing on paper.

Photographic images can be employed in any situation where communication is involved. A company's annual report and accounts is normally a somewhat dry affair, at least on statistics pages. The pencils used for the W. H. Smith report to depict a ten-year turnover graph enliven the page and help to focus on an aspect of the company's activities. A full colour photograph was used with vignetted shadows, creating the illusion of the pencils having been placed on the page. Graph treatments in these situations are generally either drawn or employ some flat graphic technique. The use of photography has the advantage of being unexpected and therefore, perhaps, more interesting.

Photography and graphic design have come a long way since Johann Schulze found that a light sensitive compound could be applied to a flat surface or Gutenberg produced his first Bible. It is not so much that technology and the resultant techniques have improved anything in the aesthetic or communication sense; rather that they have fundamentally changed the way in which we produce (and respond to) images.

The technology of phototechniques will change more rapidly in the near future than hitherto, due to the micro-chip threshold having been crossed and the resultant revolution in various computer controlled imagery; awareness of these changes and their potential is and will continue to be a prerequisite for everyone concerned with visual communication.